Utterances
of Shaikh ʿAbd al-Qādir al-Jīlānī

(Malfūẓāt)

Utterances
of Shaikh ʿAbd al-Qādir al-Jīlānī

(Malfūẓāt)

TRANSLATED FROM THE ARABIC BY MUHTAR HOLLAND

AL-BAZ PUBLISHING, INC.
HOUSTON, TEXAS

"All upon the earth shall pass away" Qur'ān (55:26)

Cover calligraphy: Rohana Filippi

Using watercolor and wax to combine the beauty of Arabic script with the Qur'ānic message on paper, Italian artist Rohana Filippi has developed her own artistic style through personal research and inner inspiration. Her art is entirely devoted to "expressing Allāh's presence everywhere," and as such her paintings offer an opportunity to enjoy a harmonious, universal experience that transcends all cultural and religious barriers. Ms. Filippi, who currently resides in Colombia, has lived and worked in England, Mexico, and the United States.

Cover Design: Dryden Design, Houston, Texas

Body text set entirely in Jilani font by Al-Baz Publishing, Inc.

Printed on acid-free paper

Library of Congress
Catalog Card Number: 92-73637

ISBN: 1-882216-03-2

Published by Al-Baz Publishing, Inc.
P.O. Box 672671, Houston, TX 77267-2671
(800) 578-7409

Printed and bound in the United States of America

Contents

Publisher's Preface **vii**
Acknowledgments **ix**
Translator's Introduction **xi**

Utterances 5–132
Obituary of the Shaikh 133
Concerning the Author, Shaikh ʿAbd al-Qādir al-Jīlānī 137
About the Translator 143

Publisher's Preface

The words of Shaikh 'Abd al-Qādir al-Jīlānī can undoubtedly be considered among the most precious treasures of Islām. Indeed, Al-Baz Publishing was founded with the intention of providing fine English translations of his works for the benefit of English-speaking Muslims everywhere, in the spirit of wishing to share the benefit and blessing we have received ourselves at his hand.

I first became interested in Shaikh 'Abd al-Qādir in learning from my own spiritual guide and benefactor Bapak Muhammad Sumohadiwidjojo, founder of the Subud brotherhood (may Allāh be well pleased with him), that Allāh had bestowed on the Shaikh the same opening and contact that Bapak himself received from Allāh, and which he has passed on to us.

Anyone familiar with the *latihan kejiwaan* of Subud will understand that to be so honored by Almighty God is an unusual occurrence in the history of mankind, such grace usually being bestowed on very few of His creatures. My interest thus being aroused, I sought out the surviving manuscripts from their various repositories around the world, and began the task of having them translated. From the very first reading it was apparent to me that what Bapak had said about the Shaikh was true.

O reader! This endeavor is for you! If you find benefit in the reading of these talks, pray that Allāh bless the Shaikh, and pray for us too, that our offering may find acceptance in His sight!

Ruslan Moore
Al-Baz Publishing, Inc.
December, 1992

Acknowledgments

All praise is due to Allāh, the Beneficent, the Merciful!

We bear witness that there is no god except Allāh, and that Muhammad is the Messenger of Allāh!

Our Lord, thank You for giving us this wholesome task!

Grateful thanks to Muhtar Holland for devoting years of his life to translating these works; may Allāh bless him! Thanks too, to the many who have helped make this publication possible, among them the following.

Salim al-din Quraishi of the British India Office Library, London
Dr. Hars Kurio of the Staatsbibliothek Preussischer Kulturbesitz, Berlin
Husein Rofé for "Reflections on Subud"
Lateef Ismail for his part
Rohana Woodward for the clue
Fardiyah Moore, my wife, for her support
Marius Moore for his help
Ridwan Lowther for research and for style and font assistance
Liliana Gardner for design fundamentals
Frances Gardner for the flowers
Rohana Filippi for the cover art
Susannah Ortego for coordinating the production

Translator's Introduction[1]

To the reader who is approaching these *Utterances of Shaikh 'Abd al-Qādir al-Jīlānī* from the standpoint of familiarity with *Revelations of the Unseen* and *The Sublime Revelation,* one feature will be conspicuous by its absence from the text: In the work presented here, there is no division into numbered Discourses, let alone any indication of where and when the words of the Shaikh (may Allāh be well pleased with him) were uttered and recorded. Our editors have attempted to compensate for this, to some extent, by using typographical devices to highlight any obvious interruption in the flow of the text, such as a note to the effect that a question was raised by a member of the Shaikh's audience.

As for the time and place of these *Utterances,* it is safe to assume that they were delivered at the Shaikh's residence and guesthouse in Baghdād, or in the adjacent schoolhouse, during approximately the same period as the talks recorded in *The Sublime Revelation.* In the latter work (entitled *al-Fatḥ ar-Rabbānī* in the original Arabic), known to have been compiled by the Shaikh's son 'Abd ar-Razzāq, we find each of the Discourses prefaced by a heading, informing us where and precisely when the session *[majlis]* was held, from the first ("in the guesthouse *[ribāṭ],* in the early morning of Sunday, 3rd of Shawwāl, A.H. 545") to the sixty-second and last ("in the schoolhouse *[madrasa],* in the early morning of Friday, the last day of Rajab, A.H. 546"). These Islamic dates fall within the period 1150–1152 C.E.

[1] For more general background information, including an explanation of the names and titles of Shaikh 'Abd al-Qādir, a short account of his life in Baghdād, and a brief survey of his literary works, please refer to p. 137, where the editor has reproduced a slightly modified version of the Translator's Introduction to *Revelations of the Unseen,* a companion volume in this series.

Apart from the obvious similarities in style and content, we can support our assumption by pointing to the fact that these collected *Utterances* (called *Malfūẓāt* in Arabic) have frequently been treated as a kind of appendix or supplement to both older manuscript and modern printed editions of *al-Fatḥ ar-Rabbānī*. In the version issued by the Damascus publisher Dār al-Albāb (undated, but clearly recent), the entire contents of the *Malfūẓāt* are added directly at the end of *al-Fatḥ ar-Rabbānī,* with no separate heading, so that the sixty-second session appears to occupy more than fifty pages of densely printed Arabic text! Voluble as the blessed Shaikh may have been when occasion demanded, he would surely have been hard pressed to utter so many words of profound wisdom in the early morning of Friday, the last day of Rajab, A.H. 546. There can be little doubt, however, that he did indeed utter his *Malfūẓāt* not long before and/or after that date.

In the Pakistani edition (*Fuyūḍ-i Yazdānī,* [Urdu] translation of *al-Fatḥ ar-Rabbānī*. Karachi: Madīna Publishing Co., 1989), a manuscript text has been reproduced by phototypography. It is interesting to note that the editor, while applying the heading *Malfūẓāt* to the Urdu translation of the appendix containing the Shaikh's *Utterances,* has preferred the caption *al-Futūḥāt* for the Arabic text, which is presented alongside the Urdu. Whether or not there is any traditional basis for this title, it is far from inappropriate. The Arabic word *Futūḥāt* is the plural of *Futūḥ* (as in *Futūḥ al-Ghaib,* the original title of the Shaikh's *Revelations of the Unseen*). Moreover, *Futūḥ* is itself the plural of *Fatḥ* (as in *al-Fatḥ ar-Rabbānī,* the original title of the Shaikh's *Sublime Revelation*).[2] Thanks to the peculiar genius of the Arabic language, with its plural and superplural formations, it is thus possible to emphasize the revelatory character of all the recorded utterances that have come down to us from Shaikh 'Abd al-Qādir al-Jīlānī (may Allāh the

[2] For a more extensive discussion of the Arabic root *F-T-Ḥ* and its ramifications of meaning in the many words derived from it, including the terms *Fatḥ, Futūḥ* and *Futūḥāt,* the reader is referred to the Translator's Introduction to *The Sublime Revelation* (translation of *al-Fatḥ ar Rabbānī,* published by Al-Baz).

Exalted be well pleased with him). To many of our readers, the use of the term *Futūḥāt* in this context will also be reminiscent of its occurrence in *al-Futūḥāt al-Makkiyya* [The Meccan Revelatory Disclosures], the title of a famous work by Shaikh Ibn al-'Arabī (may Allāh bestow His mercy upon him).

Our readers may also come to share the view of this translator, who has found the contents of the *Utterances of Shaikh 'Abd al-Qādir al-Jīlānī*—whatever their proper title in Arabic—to be in many respects the most revealing of all the works attributed to the Shaikh himself, or written by his later biographers. It is not for me, of course, to impose my own impressions. If I have been blessed with success in my endeavor to let the author use the very words in which he would have expressed himself in the English language, our readers will be qualified to reach their personal conclusions. Let me confine myself, therefore, to just a few observations:

Here we encounter the Shaikh at his most frankly outspoken. "O alien to the human race," he exclaims at one point. "O straggler from the ranks of the champions of truth and the Lord's own people! Do you not realize that I am your goldsmith's furnace, your probe and your touchstone? Do your utmost. Refuse to let me eat from your plate. Unsheathe your sword against me.... I am giving you good advice and treating you with compassion. I am afraid that you may die an atheist, a pretender, an impostor—doomed to suffer in your grave the punishment of the hypocrites.... You will soon be dead. There is no hostility between me and you. You will have cause to remember what I am saying to you."

In addition to reporting the Shaikh's words, the recorder has treated us to many intriguing descriptions of his state and behavior in the presence of those who attended his meetings. For instance: "The Shaikh (may Allāh be well pleased with him) was deep in his state of rapture *[samā']* and ecstasy *[wajd]*, when he was handed a slip of paper with a question concerning a point of Islamic jurisprudence written on it. He said: 'I must ask you to wait until I get permission to speak on the subject, and while I see what occurs to me.'" At one point, we are told: "He blew into his hand, and turned his face in all directions." Once, in the course of responding to a question, "he leaned against the lectern, resting his head on his hand and closing his eyes...." On another occasion, to quote one of the most striking passages of all:

> Just then, a sparrow came and settled on his head; so he bowed his head for it. He stayed in that position, with the bird on his head and the people on the stairs of the lectern. He did not stir until one of his companions held out his hand toward it and it flew away. Then he offered a prayer of supplication. The people were making a great commotion with their weeping, supplications and professions of repentance. He stepped down and went out immediately to the congregational mosque *[jāmi']* of ar-Ruṣāfa, followed by a great throng of people, amid a scene of weeping, screaming, ecstasy *[wajd]* and the shedding of clothes. Then he said (may Allāh be well pleased with him): "This is the end of the age. O Allāh, we take refuge with You from the evil thereof!"

Since we are likely to find ourselves wondering, as is surely quite natural, about the kind of impact the Shaikh's bluntness could have had on his listeners, it is both enlightening and reassuring to come across the following passage:

> When the Shaikh had stepped down from the lectern, one of his pupils said to him: "You were quite extreme in your admonition, and you spoke to [that person] very harshly!" But the Shaikh replied: "If my words have had any effect upon him, he will surely come back for more." (The man did in fact attend the meeting regularly from then on. He would also visit the Shaikh at other times, outside the formal session, and always behaved with the utmost humility and modesty in his presence. May Allāh the Exalted bestow His mercy upon him).

There are many helpful clues for those of us who are curious about the composition of the Shaikh's audience, such as: "Present...on this occasion was the superintendent of the household of...the son of the Commander-in-Chief, accompanied by numerous servants and attendants.... When he made his entrance, the Shaikh (may Allāh be well pleased with him) said: 'You are all serving one another. Allāh—who will serve Him?... Spread your wealth around. You are merely a traveler passing through.'" — "One day a funeral procession came in during his meeting...."

Finally, one can hardly fail to note the remarkable topicality of many passages in this work, considering that it dates from over eight hundred years ago. I was editing my translation during an American Presidential election campaign in which the watchword was: "The economy—stupid!" The reader will surely hear an echo of the spontaneous chuckle (not too irreverent, I trust) which I emitted when rereading the lines: "Economic inflation is the King's whip, which He uses to administer corrective punishment. (The Shaikh said this at a time of severe hardship and austerity.)"

Dear fellow travelers, passing through, I leave you now to make your own discoveries. May Allāh Most Generous reward you with treasures of great worth, both outwardly and inwardly. Āmīn.

Muhtar Holland

Utterances
of Shaikh ʿAbd al-Qādir al-Jīlānī

(Malfūẓāt)

بِسْمِ ٱللَّهِ ٱلرَّحْمَٰنِ ٱلرَّحِيمِ

Allāh! There is no god but He! (Qur'ān 2:255)

SHAIKH Muḥyi'd-dīn Abū Muḥammad 'Abd al-Qādir (may Allāh be well pleased with him) said:

When 'Alī ibn al-Fuḍail ibn 'Iyāḍ[1] died, his father saw him in a dream, so he asked him: "How has Allāh treated you?"

"O my father," he said, "I do not see how the servant could have anything better than his Lord."

O my dear son, Allāh is the only One you need. Do not concern yourself with any other. The whole universe belongs to Him *[ad-dār dāruhu]*, and the means of subsistence *[arzāq]* are His creation.

> He ordained therein its various forms of sustenance. (41:10)

The angels *[malā'ika]* are fed on your means of subsistence. All that is good comes from Him, and all that is bad comes from Him. He shoots at the servant with the arrows of misfortunes, but then, when the servant shuts his eyes in the face of the shooting, along comes the physician of nearness *[qurb]* to treat his wounds, the physician of love *[ḥubb]* to lift him up, and the physician of ardent longing *[shawq]* to embrace him. The process begins with unpleasant adversities. If the Garden [of Paradise] is hedged around with unpleasant adversities, how is it likely to be in the case of nearness to the Lord of Truth (Almighty and Glorious is He)? The believer *[mu'min]* is the King's agent *['āmil]* in the village of this world.

[1] Abū 'Alī ibn al-Fuḍail ibn 'Iyāḍ at-Tālaqānī died in Mecca in A.H. 187/803 C.E. Born in Khurāsān, he is said to have been a highwayman at the beginning of his career. After his conversion he went to Kūfa, where he studied under Sufyān ath-Thawrī and achieved considerable repute as an authority on the Traditions of the Prophet (Allāh bless him and give him peace). He is famous for his bold preaching before the Caliph Hārūn ar-Rashīd, who called him "the Prince of the Muslims." It is said that when he died sorrow disappeared from the world.

When the innermost being *[sirr]* becomes a heaven and the heart *[qalb]* an earth, He lets the heart share the banquet *[sūr]* of the heaven of the innermost being. If He so wills, He brings the two of them together.

Then the Shaikh (may the mercy of Allāh be upon him) saw a vision close by, and he stretched out his hand as if he were hugging something. Then he said:

O you people who are here for this meeting *[majlis]*, please excuse us. I am subject to the restrictions imposed by circumstance, to the restrictions imposed by life. Today I am dumb, I am deaf.

I saw my father Adam (peace be upon him) and he said: "O my dear son, you have restored my family line *[nasab]* to spiritual good health."

Lonely isolation is something you are bound to experience. When death befalls you, every close friend will cut you off and every relative will part company with you, so part company with them and cut them off before they leave you in the lurch. Then the grave will be a pathway to the Lord of Truth (Almighty and Glorious is He), a corridor *[dihlīz]*. You must die before you die *[mut qabla an tamūta]*. Die to you and to them, then you will live in Him. You will become like a dead man, who is fed and manipulated by the hand of predestination *[sābiqa]*, receiving his allotted shares disinterestedly. When this process is complete, along will come life in the nearness of Allāh (Almighty and Glorious is He) and knowledge *['ilm]* of Him. This bird will take off, not caring whether the Resurrection has occurred or has not occurred, whether death has been created or has not been created, for his sole concern is arriving at the Truth *[Ḥaqq]*.

As for the rules of law *[aḥkām]*, they must be kept and preserved. Glory be to Him who has covered you with the protection of the law *[ḥukm]*, and has uncovered your vision by means of knowledge *['ilm]*.

One of you may dress up in the apparel of the righteous *[ṣāliḥūn]*, in gray and coarse wool *[ṣūf]*, yet in our eyes he is an unbeliever *[kāfir]*.

The servant [of Allāh] may feed himself from his earnings while his faith is growing strong, then it will become unlawful *[yuḥarramu]* for him to feed himself from his earnings. He will be told: "Open the treasure house of creative power *[takwīn]*. Take from the treasure houses of knowledge *['ilm]*."

As the Prophet (may Allāh the Exalted bless him and give him peace) has said:

> Free yourselves from worldly cares, as far as you can.

Make a frequent practice of remembering death and what lies beyond it, and the narrow bridge *[ṣirāṭ]* and what lies beyond it. Remember the hereafter with its bliss and its torment. Become detached from this world by concentrating on Allāh (Almighty and Glorious is He), by purifying your hearts and innermost beings *[asrār]*, by struggling against your lower selves *[nufūs]* and waging war on the devils *[shayāṭīn]*. Be liberated for the sake of Allāh (Exalted is He) and devote yourselves wholly to Him.

To affirm the Divine Unity *[tawḥīd]* is to wipe out all created beings, to move away from the upheaval of your ordinary nature *[ṭab']* toward the nature of the angels, then to pass beyond the nature of the angels and become connected to your Lord (Almighty and Glorious is He).

He gives you to drink whatever He gives you to drink, and He pays special attention to deeds performed in His sight, more than to external behavior. Islām is external *[ẓāhir]* and faith *[īmān]* is its driving force *[quwwa]*. Then real experience *[ma'rifa]* of Allāh (Almighty and Glorious is He) comes after that, then existence *[wujūd]* because of Allāh (Exalted is He), for when your very existence is because of Him, the whole of you belongs to Him.

The believer *[mu'min]* feeds himself from his earnings *[kasb]* and his material means *[sabab]*, acknowledging that it all comes from Allāh (Almighty and Glorious is He). Then, when he has grown stronger [in his faith], he gets his food through his absolute trust *[tawakkul]*. He still sees it as coming from Allāh (Almighty and Glorious is He); his former attitude to this remains unchanged. Even if he were to sit in the River Tigris for a thousand years, his heart would remain attached to Allāh (Almighty and Glorious is He).

Be warned—may Allāh have mercy on you!—about how it will be when you meet Him, since you challenge Him concerning His judgment *[qaḍā']* and His decree *[qadar]*. Do not challenge and do not argue. Ezra *['Uzair]* challenged his Lord (Almighty and Glorious is He) on the subject of creation, questioning whether He could create something and then make it cease to exist, so He erased him from the register *[dīwān]* of Prophethood *[nubuwwa]*. He caused him to die for a hundred years, an exile from His presence, then He brought him back to life and restored him to his former condition.

Make praying for forgiveness *[istighfār]* the regular practice of your tongue, grateful acknowledgment *[i'tirāf]* the regular practice of your heart, and quiet calm *[sukūn]* the regular practice of your innermost being *[sirr]*. Remembrance *[dhikr]* is first made with the tongue, then it moves in deeper to reach the heart. Loves comes along, and ardent longing *[shawq]* moves back out to reach the tongue.

I have been in the company of Shaikhs, and not once did I see the white of their teeth tucking into good food without their giving me a morsel to eat; they were too courteous to behave like that. Let others eat their fill, while you go hungry. Let others enjoy respect, while you remain humble. Let others become rich, while you remain poor. It is only for this that I am training you, preparing you and teaching you.

Today I am positively convinced that you can neither bring me any benefit nor cause me any harm, that you can neither add anything to my sustenance nor subtract one atom from it. Once that was clear, I could address my words to you. I grasped the truth of this while I was in the deserts and the wastelands.

Indulging the appetites of the flesh will harden the heart, restrict the innermost being *[sirr]*, eliminate keen intelligence *[fiṭna]*, cause an increase in sleepiness and negligence, intensify greed and extend expectations.

O prisoner in the prison of your passions *[hawā]*! O slave of creatures! O you who are ignorant of the ultimate outcome of your state of affairs! O you who are ignorant of creatures and of the Lord of Truth (Almighty and Glorious is He), of what you owe and of what is due to you! If you do not understand, at least have the sense to remember death. Remembering death is the key to all that is good and to salvation *[salāma]*. If you remember death, you will no longer be guilty of such excesses. If your greediness gets weaker and your expectations diminish, you will realize that we all belong to Allāh, and to Him we are all returning *[istarja'ta]*;[2] you will delegate all your affairs to Allāh (Almighty and Glorious is He).

O young man! There can be no salvation *[falāḥ]* for you until you acknowledge His blessings, and those blessings immerse you in the realization of His Oneness *[tawḥīd]*, and then in the realization of His Oneness you pass beyond noticing anything other than Him. Why should He love someone who complains about Him, argues with Him and quarrels with Him? Love *[ḥubb]* and ardent longing *[shawq]* and nearness *[qurb]* to Him do not become established under these conditions. If loving affection *[maḥabba]* is genuine, no pain is felt when the decrees of destiny *[aqdār]* come into effect. When loving affection is firmly installed, resistance and suspicion disappear.

Every step you take is a step toward the grave. You are on a journey to the grave.

One of the righteous has said: "He who really knows *['ārif]* is too preoccupied with the One he knows *[ma'rūf]* to be concerned with acceptance or rejection, praise or blame."

When the lower self *[nafs]* passes away, its place is taken by the commandment of Allāh. When this world passes away, its place is taken by the hereafter. When the hereafter passes away, its place is taken by the nearness of Allāh (Almighty and Glorious is He). In His nearness one feels at home and can relax in comfort.

[2] The verb *istarja'a* (from the root *r-j-'*) means to make the affirmation: *innā lillāhi wa-innā ilaihi rāji'ūn*—"Surely we belong to Allāh, and surely to Him we are returning."

Performing the prayer *[ṣalāt]* will take you halfway along the path, keeping the fast *[ṣawm]* will set you at the door, and charitable giving *[ṣadaqa]* will admit you inside the palace. One of the Shaikhs has said as much: "To cover the distance along the path to Allāh, you must seek the help of patience *[ṣabr]* and prayer *[ṣalāt]*."

He who takes the route of "it does not exist" *[sāliku laisa]*, how lonely is he, what a stranger is he!

But for the safeguard of the law *[ḥukm]*, the slanderer of Joseph (peace be upon him) would announce all your secrets and your doings, but the law clings to the hem of knowledge *['ilm]*, appealing to it for protection so that it does not become public knowledge.

It may happen that someone abstains from the blessing *[ni'ma]* because of preoccupation with the Benefactor *[Mun'im]*, and he may be deprived of the blessing so that he cannot be distracted by it, for if he continues to devote all his attention to Him, He will draw him near to Himself and will put creative power *[takwīn]* at his disposal.

My words are from beyond you, beyond where I lose sight of you, therefore I have transcended this world of yours and I have transcended the hereafter.

I have looked at you and seen that you have no power to cause harm or to bring benefit, to give or to withhold. Allāh is the One who operates you *[Mutaṣarrif fīkum]*. You cause harm only after the harmful action of Allāh (Almighty and Glorious is He), so I attribute it all to Allāh. As for this world, I have seen that it is transitory, fleeting, passing, murderous and treacherous, so I dismiss with scorn the idea of placing trust in it and becoming attached to it, since it passes away so quickly. And as for the hereafter, I paused there for a while. I examined its condition and its flaw became apparent to me, namely the fact that it is an invented entity *[muḥdatha]* having features in common *[mushtarika]* [with this world]. I saw that Allāh has made provision in it for the desire of the self *[nafs]* "and all that eyes find sweet," to quote His words (Almighty and Glorious is He):

> And therein is all that selves *[anfus]* desire and eyes find sweet. (43:71)

I said, "So where is the heart's desire?" Then I turned away from it toward its Master *[Mawlā]*, its Maker *[Bāri']*, its Creator *[Khāliq]* and its Inventor *[Muḥdith]*.

When the servant is conscientiously devoted to Allāh (Almighty and Glorious is He), He rewards him by converting ignorance into knowledge *['ilm]*, remoteness into nearness, silence into spoken recognition, loneliness into intimate friendship *[uns]*, and darkness into light.

If you want satisfaction from me, O lower self *[nafs]*, O passions *[hawā]*, O natural impulses *[ṭab']*, O willfulness *[irāda]*, you must be content with the affirmation of Divine Unity *[tawḥīd]*, detachment from all created beings, reliance on Allāh (Almighty and Glorious is He) and ceasing to pay attention to creatures. I will not take a crumb from them without first paying attention to the Truth *[Ḥaqq]*; otherwise I have sworn that I shall neither eat nor drink, for when you die I shall fly with my innermost being *[sirr]* to the Lord of Truth (Almighty and Glorious is He).

The walls of the religion *[dīn]* of our Prophet have come tumbling down; they are crying out for help, for someone to rebuild it. Its river has run dry. The Lord is not worshipped, or if He is worshipped at all He is worshipped as an outward show and hypocritically. Who will lend a hand to reconstruct the walls, to get the river current flowing, and to smash the experts in hypocrisy? I am speaking of a kind of knowledge *['ilm]* which we cannot express in plain words, and which we cannot teach to an angel *[malak]* who will not pass it on to anybody.

The Mount *[aṭ-Ṭūr]* is your heart; no devil *[shaiṭān]* can see it to corrupt it, nor any worldly ruler *[sulṭān]* to conquer it. Allāh (Exalted is He) has sworn by the Mount (52:1) in order to confide in His beloved friend *[ḥabīb]* and interlocutor *[kalīm]*, [Moses] (peace be upon him), and to make Himself manifest to him. When the heart really knows *['arafa]* the Lord of Truth (Almighty and Glorious is He), He expands it until it encompasses the jinn, the human race and the angels, and then, when there is nothing left to distract its attention from Him, He draws it near and brings it close [to Himself].

Surely you must have heard of the staff of Moses and how it swallowed up all those loads of sticks and ropes without undergoing any alteration?

Question: Kāmil the Sailor *[al-Mallāḥ]* said to him: "Al-Ḥasan al-Baṣrī[3] has said: 'If the scholar is not a pious abstainer *[zāhid]*, he will be a torment for the people of his day and age.' Why should he be a torment for them?"

The Shaikh (may Allāh be well pleased with him) gave the following reply:

Because he will speak without sincerity *[ikhlāṣ]* and without putting his knowledge into practice, so his words will not touch their hearts. They cannot have a lasting effect, since his students will merely hear them without acting on them.

When the heart is sound and filled with the light of knowledge *['ilm]*, it uses that light to snuff out the fire of creatures' sins of disobedience, just as the Fire [of Hell] will be extinguished by the light of the believer *[mu'min]* when he passes over it.

It has been said that the corner for religious retreat *[zāwiya]* represents opposition to the lower self *[nafs]*, to carnal desires *[shahawāt]* and to creatures, mastery of the traveling companion *[rafīq]* and then the riding camel *[qa'ūd]*. Seclusion *[khalwa]* is the path of the hereafter. The lower self is not fit to be a traveling companion on the path, and this applies also to the passions *[hawā]*, for they cause one to go astray. The devil is also an enemy who is unfit for companionship. Carnal desires are bad influences that will blind the eye of your perceptive faculty along your path, and creatures are highway robbers.

[3] Al-Ḥasan ibn Abi'l-Ḥasan al-Baṣrī is revered as one of the greatest saints of early Islām. Born in Medina in A.H. 21/642 C.E., he was brought up in Baṣra, where he met many Companions of the Prophet (Allāh bless him and give him peace.) He died in A.H. 110/728 C.E.

You must leave your passions behind at the door of your private retreat *[khalwa]*, then go in all by yourself. You will get to see your friendly Companion *[mu'nis]* inside your private space.

The Disciples *[ḥawāriyyūn]* said to Jesus (peace be upon him): "Teach us the supreme knowledge *[al-'ilm al-akbar]*," so he told them: "The fear of Allāh (Almighty and Glorious is He), cheerful acceptance of the judgment *[qaḍā']* of Allāh, and love for Allāh."

You are an atheist *[zindīq]*. In private you sinfully disobey Him, then you make a public show of worshipful service *['ibāda]* and pious devotion *[zahāda]*. Do you feel safe from the ultimate outcome?

Woe unto you! Our allotted shares *[aqsām]* are in the keeping of Allāh (Exalted is He). Compare the situation of a man in Khurāsān who has a wealthy kinsman *[nasīb]* in 'Irāq. His kinsman dies, leaving no heir *[wārith]* apart from him. Will the inheritance not pass into his ownership, even though he is unaware of the fact?

You are ordinary people *[qawm 'awāmm]*. It is appropriate to talk to you about food and drink and what to wear, but the commandment overwhelms us, so we must speak of other subjects.

The heart must eliminate the materiality *[māddiyya]* of the lower self *[nafs]*, so that you can use it as a vehicle for your journey back to Allāh (Almighty and Glorious is He).

If your heart happens to feel love for one person and hatred for another, what are you to do? Should you love because of your natural inclination *[ṭab']* and hate because of your natural inclination? That would be unworthy. You must rub the whole matter against the touchstones of the Book and the Sunna. If it is in conformity with these two, [well and good]; otherwise you must reject it. If the verdict is in favor of its being correct, refer back to your heart.

When the heart puts the Book and the Sunna into practice, it draws near [to the Lord]. When it draws near, it gets to know *['alima]*, and when it knows it recognizes what is due to it and what is required of it, what is due to the Truth and what to falsehood, what is due to Satan *[ash-Shaiṭān]* and what to the All-Merciful *[ar-Raḥmān].* It can see how close it is to its Lord (Almighty and Glorious is He), and how near the Lord is to itself. It is always in a state of happiness in the company of the All-Merciful (Almighty and Glorious is He). It becomes the commercial agent *[bayyā']* of the King, buying goods and then distributing them among the people.

When you enter here, you must divest yourself of your knowledge and come in naked. By the same token you must divest yourself of your abstinence *[zuhd]*, your cautious restraint *[wara']* and your spiritual states *[aḥwāl]*, for if you enter my presence fully clothed this may get in the way of your receiving what I have to offer here. Set all that stuff aside and come on in. Take what is here and none of that will be lost to you.

I once entered the presence of a certain Shaikh while he was speaking about notions *[khawāṭir].* "Do you like this business I am in?" he asked. "Yes," I replied. Then he said: "I fast all the year round *[aṣūmu'd-dahr]* and I break my fast every morning before dawn *[ufṭiru waqta kulli saḥar].*" He also remarked: "The food in this town is not good, so try to avoid it."

Sarī as-Saqaṭī[4] used to urge al-Junaid[5] to lecture the people, then [in a dream] he saw the Prophet (Allāh bless him and give him peace) ordering him to do just that, so when he met him again he said to him: "You would not take our advice until you were given the order!"

Woe unto you! You lecture the people and after your work there is only a layer of soot *[sukhām].*

[4] Abu'l-Ḥasan Sarī ibn al-Mughallis as-Saqaṭī was the uncle and teacher of al-Junaid. Having begun his career in Baghdād as a dealer in secondhand goods, he became a pupil of Ma'rūf al-Karkhī. He died in A.H. 253/867 C.E., at the age of 98.

[5] Abu 'l-Qāsim ibn Muḥammad ibn al-Junaid al-Khazzāz al-Qawārīrī an-Nihāwandī (d. A.H. 298/910 C.E.). The son of a glass-merchant and nephew of Sarī as-Saqaṭī, he was a close associate of al-Muḥāsibī. Renowned for the clarity of his perception and the firmness of his self-control, he earned a reputation as the principal exponent of the "sober" school of Islāmic mysticism. His *Rasā'il* [Epistles] consist of letters to private individuals, and short tractates on mystical themes, some cast in the form of commentaries on Qur'ānic texts.

There is no one upon the face of the earth that I am afraid of, or on whom I pin my hopes, and there is no such person in heaven, none in this world and none in the hereafter, apart from the Lord of Truth (Almighty and Glorious is He).

Someone asked a certain righteous man, "Do you see your Lord?" and he said in reply: "If I did not see Him, my whole state of being would fall apart." When the enquirer asked, "How do you see Him?" he went on to say: "One must close the eyes of his physical existence, then he will see his Lord, just as He shows Himself to the people in the Garden [of Paradise]. As He wills, he will see His heart, he will see His attributes *[ṣifāt]*, he will see His beneficence *[iḥsān]*, he will see His gracious favor *[luṭf]*, he will see His kindness *[birr]* and he will see His protecting wing *[kanaf]*."

Abū'l-Qāsim al-Junaid (may Allāh be well pleased with him) used to say: "What do I care about me?"

The Ṣūfī is one whose heart is pure *[ṣafā]*, free from attachment to his physical existence *[wujūd]*. His heart is an ambassador between him and his Lord (Almighty and Glorious is He). He cannot be a Ṣūfī until he sees his Prophet (Allāh bless him and give him peace) in his dreams, educating him, telling him what to do and what not to do. His heart will make progress and his innermost being *[sirr]* will be purified *[yaṣfū]* at the door of the King, while his hand is in the hand of the Prophet (Allāh bless him and give him peace).

The first words spoken by Adam (peace be upon him) were in Syriac *[suryānī]*, and people will be examined in Syriac on the Day of Resurrection. Then, when they enter the Garden [of Paradise], they will speak in Arabic, in the language of Muḥammad (Allāh bless him and give him peace).

One of the righteous has said: "If the servant obeys Allāh (Exalted is He), He will grant him real knowledge *[ma'rifa]*, and if he then disobeys Him, He will not deprive him of it, so that He may bring it in evidence against him on the Day of Resurrection."

The angel's notion *[khāṭir al-malak]* will come and make its presence felt in the heart of the believer *[mu'min]*, so he must pause beside it and ask it: "Who are you and where do you come from?" Then it will say: "I am your portion of Prophethood *[nubuwwa]* from the Truth *[Ḥaqq]*. I am the Truth. I come from the Friend *[Ḥabīb]*, I come from the Companion *[Rafīq]*." This notion will fill his inner being *[bāṭin]*, his hearing and his sight. You will see him becoming fond of solitude, emigrating from his native land. Then another command will come to him, to make him somewhat disturbed. Then yet another command will come to him, also causing disturbance, until calm eventually arrives. When calm has arrived, conversation will go on constantly. You will see him apparently lending his ear to someone at his side, as if someone is engaging him in conversation.

A man got up to request some worldly favor, so the Shaikh made him sit down and said:

I am instructing you to practice abstinence from this world, then from the hereafter, and then you may ask Allāh (Exalted is He). You must abstain to the point where the Lord of Truth (Almighty and Glorious is He) offers you something and you do not take it.

Allāh (Almighty and Glorious is He) conveyed through inspiration *[awḥā]* to Jesus (blessing and peace be upon him): "O Jesus, be careful not to let Me slip away from you."

Moses (blessings and peace be upon him) said to his Lord (Almighty and Glorious is He): "O my Lord, give me some recommendation." Said He: "I recommend Me to you." Then he said again: "Give me some recommendation." Again He said: "I recommend Me to you." This exchange was repeated four times, and each time He said: "I recommend Me to you."

There is nothing worth talking about, until you have been hatched out of the egg of your worldly existence *[wujūd]* and embraced by the wing of the sacred law *[shar']*. At that point the bird call will have an effect on you, and you will gather the seeds of grace *[faḍl]* and acquire a taste for it. (By this the Shaikh means that one should give up the idea of lecturing people and inviting them to

Allāh (Almighty and Glorious is He), until one experiences an attraction to it coming from Allāh, and has the aptitude for speaking to people and summoning them to Allāh (Almighty and Glorious is He).)

Master this outer law *[ḥukm ẓāhir]* by putting it into practice, then look and see how good it is to enjoy His nearness and His intimate conversation *[munājāt]*.

Ordinary folk are great fanciers of food *[al-'awāmm li'ṭ-ṭa'ām 'ushshāq]*.

As I am speaking, you are a nonentity in my sight. Heaven and earth are also a nonentity in my sight. None can bring me any benefit or cause me any harm, except Allāh (Almighty and Glorious is He).

Question: What is the meaning of the saying of a certain Shaikh: "Catch the seeker *[murīd]* before he becomes aware"?

The Shaikh (may Allāh be well pleased with him) said in response:

That is to say, catch him while he is engaged in worshipful service *['ibāda]* and working hard at prayer *[ṣalāt]* and fasting *[ṣiyām]*, before he becomes aware of His nearness and His gracious favor, for if He draws him near and treats him kindly, he will take his practice less seriously, before he is really aware of the juice and the courses of food you have to offer. He will wish to follow that path and leave you behind.

Every one of them is distracted by some preoccupation: This one is the slave of his social status *[jāh]*, while this one is the slave of his worldly ruler *[sulṭān]* and this other is the slave of his lower self *[nafs]* and his wardrobe. Every one of them is preoccupied with something: This one with his fasting *[ṣiyām]* and his prayers *[ṣalāt]*, this one with his reporting of traditions *[riwāya]*, this one with his fear of people and this other with his love of the Garden [of

Paradise]. There exists but one individual whose heart is devoted to Allāh (Almighty and Glorious is He), who is with Allāh, attached to Allāh and detached from creatures; he champions the cause of His religion *[dīn]*. Scour the earth, and if you find this individual, hang on to him tight.

[At first] the believer's cheerfulness shows in his face, while his sadness remains hidden in his heart, but then this is reversed so that his sadness comes to show in his face, while his cheerfulness is hidden in his heart. The sadness shows in his face for the edification of his fellow creatures, while the cheerfulness in his heart is there in the face of fate and destiny *[al-qaḍā' wa'l-qadar]*, at both of which he laughs and both of which he welcomes cheerfully.

[As the Prophet (Allāh bless him and give him peace) has said:]

> This world is the believer's prison *[ad-dunyā sijnu'l-mu'min]*.

It is his prison as long as he is just a believer, but if he perseveres in his dutiful devotion *[taqwā]*, he will be taken out of it; he will be released from his prison, from his straitened circumstances.

> Whoever is dutiful toward Allāh, He prepares a way out for him, and provides for him from sources he could never imagine. (65:2,3)

He will be hatched out of the egg of his worldly existence. He will gather the seeds of the law *[ḥukm]*. The wing of nearness will embrace and enfold him. He will be the owner of the dishes and the owner of the banquet table.

O stupid fool, all you have to offer is a flash of lightning with no staying power. All you have is a random chance; no sooner does it come than it is gone. You need to fade away and die a thousand times, then at last you will stand firm. As the night follows the day, you will endure and undergo no change. You will grow and generously spread your protective shade, after you become a prop *[watad]* for the seven earths.

Do not engage in senseless jabber. Do not make pretentious claims. A mosquito bites you and that is the end of the world as far as you are concerned. A morsel is missing from your dinner and that is the end of the world in your eyes. Let the lawful wife *[ḥālla]* enter inside you and marry your heart, then you will have baby birds that will fly up and settle on the staircase of your innermost being *[sirr]*. You will travel East and West, over land and sea.

You are asleep, and as the Prophet (Allāh bless him and give him peace) has said:

> People are asleep, but when they die they will come to their senses.

How wretched is the man who wakes up only after death! The spiritual pauper *[faqīr]* must gird his loins with contentment and wear the robe of virtuous restraint *['iffa]*, until he attains to the Lord of Truth (Almighty and Glorious is He). He must run with the feet of sincerity *[ṣidq]* in search of the door of nearness [to the Lord], hurrying away from both this world and the hereafter, hurrying away from creatures and worldly existence *[wujūd]*. He will be met by the providential care *['ināya]* of the Lord of Truth, by His compassion *[ra'fa]*, His mercy *[raḥma]*, His ardent yearning *[shawq]* for him, His raptures *[jadhabāt]*, His affectionate glances *[naẓarāt]* and His vauntings *[muhāhāt]*, as well as by the retinues of the spirits *[arwāḥ]* of His Prophets *[anbiyā']* and His angels *[malā'ika]*. The angels will keep him company and the spirits of the Prophets *[nabiyyūn]* and Messengers *[mursalūn]* will conduct him in solemn procession to the Lord of Truth.

O you who are dead in your hearts, your quest for the Garden [of Paradise] is what keeps you away from the Lord of Truth. Desist, desist! Come back, come back! You must reduce your expectations until your heart draws near, until your innermost being *[sirr]* is purified of creatures and comes close to the Lord of Truth, and you can read your prerecorded destiny *[sābiqa]*. Then you will study it line by line, word by word and letter by letter, learning about your times, your periods, your hours and your moments, and it will become clear to you where your ultimate destination lies.

Whenever fear attracts you to Him, nearness draws Him close to you, then there is constancy *[thabāt]*.

Never mind whether your life be long or short, whether the Resurrection be at hand or not, whether people love you or hate you, give you things or deprive you of them...

At this point the Shaikh stood up shouting, covered his face and then uncovered it. Then he said:

> O fire, be coolness and peace for Abraham. (21:69)

O Allāh, do not publish our reports!

Then he sat down again.

Sufyān ath-Thawrī[6] said to Fuḍail ibn 'Iyāḍ[7] (may Allāh be well pleased with them both): "Come here and let us weep over the foreknowledge Allāh has about us," for they were fearful and wary.

> They give that which they give with hearts afraid. (23:60)

They were afraid that their deeds might not be accepted. They were afraid of coming to a bad end *[sū' al-khātima]*.

Imām Aḥmad [ibn Ḥanbal][8] (may Allāh be well pleased with him) used to say: "There is nothing to it but clothes that are not real clothes *[libās dūna libās]*, a meal that is not a real meal *[ṭa'ām dūna ṭa'ām]*, and a few short days."

O young man! Shut the door to the good will of creatures, then the door to the good will of the Lord of Truth will be opened unto you.

[6] Abū 'Abdillāh Sufyān ibn Sa'īd ath-Thawrī was born in Kūfa in A.H. 97/715 C.E. He founded a school of Islāmic jurisprudence *[fiqh]* which survived for about two centuries after his death in Baṣra in A.H. 161/778 C.E.

[7] See note [1] above.

[8] A prominent Traditionist and eponym of one of the four Sunnī schools of Islāmic law (d. A.H. 241/855 C.E.).

At this point the Shaikh stood up and started swaying, now to the right and then to the left, placing his hand on his chest and clutching at his breast. Then he sat down again and said:

O blind man, enter this open door! There are only two doors, one that is shut and one that is open. Enter this one that is open.

Establish a friendly relationship with the material means *[sabab]*, in accordance with the Sunna and in order to put the sacred law *[shar']* of His Prophet (Allāh bless him and give him peace) into living practice. Then advance toward the Originator *[Musabbib]* by following the Prophet (Allāh bless him and give him peace) in respect of his spiritual state *[ḥāl]*. Earning a living *[kasb]* is his Sunna, while absolute trust *[tawakkul]* is his spiritual state. Then, if you are capable of becoming extinct to you *[an tafnā 'anka]*, you must do so. [When you are attached] neither to the material means nor to the spiritual state, totally committed to the Lord of Truth, He will take care of all your needs. He will raise you up and draw you near. Indeed, He will give you more than you can ever know.

> Allāh knows, and you know not. (2:232)

Surrendering *[musalliman]* to the waves of His destiny *[qadar]*, wherever you alight you will glean *[ainamā saqaṭta laqaṭta]* the gracious favor of Allāh (Almighty and Glorious is He). Whichever way you face *[tawajjahta]*, "there is the face *[wajh]* of Allāh" (2:115). You will experience His nearness *[qurb]*, His intimate friendship *[uns]*, His kind compassion *[ra'fa]* and His mercy *[raḥma]*.

To understand the meaning of freedom from want *[ghinā]*, consider a blind man whose food is brought to him on trays. He does not know from which direction these trays come to him, but then, when he learns their source, he moves in that direction and all his needs are met. This is just how it is for this servant. When he realizes that Allāh is the One who makes things easy *[al-Musahhil]*, that He is the Giver *[al-Mu'ṭī]*, that He is the One who directs *[al-Muwajjih]* all this toward him, he attaches his heart to Allāh (Exalted is He).

Your lower self *[nafs]* is your sweetheart *[ma'shūqa]*. If only you could realize that it is in fact your enemy and your murderer, you would oppose it and refuse to give it food and drink, except for what it must have to survive; to that much it is entitled.

The corner for pious retreat *[zāwiya]* is not the proper place for you. No, the bazaars would suit you better. It is not appropriate for you to look into the secrets of Allāh (Exalted is He). One who looks into the secrets of Allāh (Exalted is He) must be able to hold his tongue. If someone cannot keep a secret, let him go into isolation from his fellow creatures. Let his dwelling be in the caves, on the beaches, in the wastelands and the deserts. If a person is incapable of respecting both the law *[ḥukm]* and knowledge *['ilm]* simultaneously, [let him do likewise].

Economic inflation *[ghalā']* is the King's whip, which He uses to adminster corrective punishment. (The Shaikh said this at a time of severe hardship and austerity.)

Woe unto you! You go seeking this world and the hereafter, yet you lay claim to love *[maḥabba]*. O stupid fool, you claim to love Him, yet you go asking Him to keep harm away and to provide only benefit. Be off with you! You are not one of the people [of the Lord], you are the slave of creatures, the slave of the lower self *[nafs]*, the passions *[hawā]* and carnal desires *[shahawāt]*. We have touchstones by which to test your coin. We have professional money changers. We have an assayer.

O pretender *[mudda'ī]*, what is this? Everything you say is out of place. Supplication *[du'ā']* has its proper place and time. Speaking is appropriate under certain conditions, while silence is appropriate under others. There is an occasion for taking notice, and another for lowering one's gaze. Where is the genuine practitioner *['āmil]*, that we may keep him company?

The champions of truth *[ṣiddīqūn]* consider it their duty to devote more and more time to worshipful service *['ibāda]*, out of gratitude to the Benefactor *[Mun'im]*. In return for His blessings they offer obedience and thanks.

While He commands you to take a little of that which is lawful *[ḥalāl]*, you must use this lawful allowance sparingly. Taking too much advantage of it will lead to your taking that which is commonly permissible *[mubāḥ]* among the Muslims, then taking this will lead to your taking that which is dubious *[shubha]*, the dubious to the unlawful *[ḥarām]*, and the unlawful to the Fire [of Hell]. The pious abstainer *[zāhid]* is one who abstains even from that which is lawful. As for abstaining from the unlawful, that is an obligatory duty *[wājib]*.

The heart may experience an ecstatic feeling *[wārid]* which it does not have the strength to bear, like when a mother screams and tears her clothes at the news of her child's death. The mind is too feeble to cope with it (meaning, with spiritual rapture *[samā']* and ecstasy *[wajd]*).

We have dealings with people in the context of prayer *[du'ā']*, and we maintain harmonious and friendly relations with them in the context of prayer, while our hearts are cool, on the lookout for the promise of Allāh, for the food of grace, until it is confirmed.

You must renounce your own will *[mashī'a]* in order to gain the will of the Lord of Truth (Almighty and Glorious is He). The prerequisites of love include giving up one's own will and volition *[tark al-mashī'a wa'l-irāda]*. As long as you are in this state, whenever your tongue makes an utterance, your ears hear and your eyes are opened, you will receive gracious favors and generous gifts. You will also receive the pure serenity of the innermost realms *[ṣafā' al-asrār]*—visible fruits and hidden gems. You will receive services *[khidam]* and servants *[khadam]*. Everything will serve you, all will praise you, and the Lord of Truth (Almighty and Glorious is He) will glory in you.

As Allāh (Almighty and Glorious is He) has said:

> Whatever the Messenger gives you, take it. Whatever he forbids you, abstain from it. (59:7)

You must carry out the commandment of Allāh and the commandment of His Messenger *[rasūl]* and put them both into practice.

On this path there is no "I" and no "We," but only "You, You."

> He is the First and the Last, the Outer and the Inner. (57:3)

The Shaikh also said (may Allāh, Exalted is He, be well pleased with him):

> By the heaven and the one who visits at night *[ṭāriq]*. (86:1)

Allāh (Almighty and Glorious is He) has sworn by the heaven and the one who visits it at night. It was visited at night by Muḥammad (Allāh bless him and give him peace). It was visited at night first by his spiritual aspiration *[himma]*, then by his physical being *[binya]*. Our Prophet (Allāh bless him and give him peace) was carried up *['urija bihi]* to the seven heavens. His Lord spoke to him and he saw Him both with the eyes in his head and with the eyes of his heart. When he was making his ascension to heaven, he saw Him on earth with the eyes of his heart, and in heaven with the eyes in his head.

When anyone has a heart that is sound, his heart will likewise see his Lord. The veils between him and heaven will be removed. The innermost beings *[asrār]* and the spiritual aspirations *[himam]* will visit by night, and the innermost beings will go on their journey.

The breasts of the champions of truth *[ṣiddīqūn]* are breasts illumined by the radiance of the mysteries of the Lord of All the Worlds *[Rabb al-'ālamīn]*.

[As the Prophet (Allāh bless him and give him peace) has said:]

> Beware of the penetrating insight of the believer *[ittaqū firāsata 'l-mu'min]*.

When the heart draws near [to the Lord], it is turned into a heaven containing the stars of knowledge *['ilm]* and the sun of real experience *[ma'rifa]*. By these radiant lights the angels find their way.

There is not one soul *[nafs]* that does not have a keeper *[ḥāfiẓ]* appointed by Allāh (Exalted is He) to keep it from falling into the clutches of the devils *[shayāṭīn]*. I have kept watch over a few individuals. They stand in rows as you keep watch over them:

> And Allāh, all unseen, surrounds them. (85:20)

You are all smooth talk and rhetoric. Your house is in ruins. You turn around and around in circles without moving from your spot, as if you were the camel at the mill. Perhaps you have been cursed by one of the saints *[awliyāʾ]* of Allāh (Exalted is He). The eyes of your perceptive faculty have gone blind. You have neglected Allāh, so Allāh has let you get lost way along the path. The eye of your intention was once firmly fixed on the roads [to your destination], then your concerns multiplied and the wings of your intention ceased to fly, so you were left as a lump of flesh between this world and the hereafter. You need a champion of the truth *[ṣiddīq]* to pray for you after the declaration of bankruptcy *[iflās]*.

The people [of the Lord] become friendly with the Lord of Truth, then with the angels *[malāʾika]*. If you make friends with these folk, another door will be opened unto you. If you cultivate the friendship of human creatures, and then have done with this, the door of friendship *[uns]* with the jinn will be opened unto you. When you have had enough of this too, the door of friendship with the angels will be opened unto you.

Things do not produce effects by themselves. Fire does not burn because of its nature *[ṭabʿ]*, nor does water irrigate because of its nature. The fire of Nimrod did not burn Abraham (blessing and peace be upon him). Abū Muslim al-Khawlānī (may the mercy of Allāh be upon him) was not burned when he was cast into the fire. The salamander is not burned by fire.

If you are sincere *[akhlaṣta]* in your works, you will be delivered *[khalaṣta]* from creatures. You will be removed from their midst. Only by getting out from amongst them will you attain to the Lord of Truth (Almighty and Glorious is He). You are seeking Him (Almighty and Glorious is He) like a man in a foreign land, who has entered a narrow pass; circling around his friend, he reaches the far end of it, then comes back to the starting point, for he is not familiar with the way through. The friend is watching him meanwhile, until, when he recognizes his bewilderment, a feeling of love comes over him, so he goes out to meet him, hugs him and enfolds him in his embrace, as Joseph did to Benjamin, for he said to him:

> I am your brother. (12:69)

Allāh has made the ground of the heart the firm resting place of real experience *[ma'rifa]* and knowledge *['ilm]*. Allāh (Almighty and Glorious is He) has three hundred and sixty glances at it between the night and the day. If He had not made it a firm resting place, it would be torn apart and ripped to shreds. When the heart becomes sound and draws close to the nearness of the Lord of Truth (Almighty and Glorious is He), He causes rivers of wisdom *[ḥikam]* to flow through it, for creatures to put to good use.

Of them [the people of the Lord] He has made firm anchors for the religion *[dīn]*. The senior rank among them is that of the Prophet (Allāh bless him and give him peace); junior to this is the rank of the Companions *[ṣaḥāba]*, and below this again is the rank of the Successors *[tābi'ūn]*. They always put what they say into practice, carrying it out in word and deed, in private and in public. The eyes of the Prophets *[nabiyyūn]* have delighted in them, and Allāh (Almighty and Glorious is He) has boasted of them to the angels. Blessed is he who follows them and relieves them of the burdens imposed by worldly needs and their dependants. [The people of the Lord are] people who have a job that keeps them too busy to earn a living, for they look after the welfare of their fellow creatures, who are like children in their eyes. They are not attached to this world. This world offers itself to them but they reject it.

This that you have in your possession does not really belong to you. It is actually the common property of the neighbors who are your partners. Your acquisitions have been placed at your disposal as a trial and a test:

> And spend out of that to which He has made you successors (57:7)—that He may see how you behave. (7:129)

Share your goods with your neighbors. Feed the poor. The home of the champion of truth *[ṣiddīq]* may look cramped, but it is very spacious inside.

Where can we find someone who shuts the door of creatures, stands at the door of the Truth and presents all his needs to his Lord? Cut off the material means *[asbāb]* and repudiate the worldly bosses *[arbāb]*, then see what you will see. Stop at His door and rest your head on the pillow of patient endurance of pain and suffering. His judgment *[qaḍā']* and His decree *[qadar]* may cut deep, but you must not complain. Then you will witness a marvel *['ajab]*. You will see how creative power *[takwīn]* can affect your spiritual state, how mercy *[raḥma]* can educate you, and how love *[maḥabba]* can accelerate your progress. The whole crux of the matter is to keep silent after the experience, for this is the opportunity for the Lord of Truth (Almighty and Glorious is He) to take pride in His servant. He declares forbidden to him the foster mothers *[marāḍi']* of creatures and material means. He restores him to His true nearness. Once he has come to be in the lap of His grace *[luṭf]*, the fragrance will satisfy him completely. The fragrance of the pain and suffering will satisfy him completely. The mercy will satisfy him completely.

> Is it not He who answers the distressed, when he calls unto Him? (27:62)

He will distress you until you call on Him in supplication. He loves urgent persistence *[ilḥāḥ]* in prayers of supplication *[du'ā']*. He will bar all the doors in your face until you come to a halt at His door. The dearly loved ones *[aḥbāb]* have seen the door of nearness opened. It is like when a mother locks her door to keep her own son out, and tells her neighbors not to leave a door open, for a purpose she wishes to achieve. He goes off and sits there weeping and feeling remorse. Whichever door he approaches, he sees that it is locked, so he comes back to his mother's door. The Lord of Truth makes things difficult for His servant, in order to bring him back to Himself and so that he will not attach his heart to creatures.

The genuine spiritual pauper *[faqīr ṣādiq]* ought not to go looking for his own sustenance *[rizq]*, but if he cannot avoid doing so altogether, he should seek just enough for his basic needs.

When He draws you near and puts you to the test, you must accept His tribulation with good grace, otherwise He will keep you fully occupied with your suffering. The craving for worldly things makes you too disturbed to experience your nearness to Allāh

(Almighty and Glorious is He) and interferes with your patient endurance of misfortune.

Anyone who does not fear Allāh (Exalted is He) must have no common sense. A town without a police force *[shiḥna]* would go to ruin. Flocks without a shepherd would be devoured. Religion *[dīn]* is fear *[khawf]*. A person who is afraid will be on the move at night; he does not stay put in one place, but keeps moving along. The goal of the travels of the people [of the Lord] is the nearness of the Lord of Truth. The journey is the journey of their hearts, the journey of their innermost beings *[asrār]*. When they arrive at the door, the innermost being *[sirr]* seeks permission to enter, and permission is granted to it. Then, after this friendly reception, it seeks permission for the heart to be admitted.

The star of the heart of the Prophet (Allāh bless him and give him peace) became a moon, the moon became a sun, what was private became public, what was inwardly concealed *[bāṭin]* became outwardly manifest *[ẓāhir]*.

The servant [of the Lord] is caught between the flood tide and the ebb tide. If he tucks his head in and stays right inside the tent of his innermost being, he will see the jewels that lie beneath the ocean, and how a hand reaches out over them, indicating to someone nearby: "You, whatever your name is, take this. And you, take that."

They [the people of the Lord] are the kings, the kings of the earth and the heaven, subject only to the Lord of Truth (Almighty and Glorious is He) by way of delegation *[niyāba]* and deputyship *[khilāfa]*. I am at the door of the King, keeping watch over them, watching them in wakefulness and in sleep.

For your sakes I put up with the insults of the people of this town. I labor patiently under all their mischief. I work night and day in sorrow and grief, considering and reconsidering. Each time I take a step forward, I am forced to step back.

Ibrāhīm ibn Ad'ham[9] once felt confused about his prayer of supplication *[du'ā']*, then his eyes were made to close and he heard

[9] Abū Isḥāq Ibrāhīm ibn Ad'ham ibn Manṣūr ibn Yazīd ibn Jābir at-Tamīmī al-'Ijlī (d. *ca.* A.H. 165/782 C.E.) was the Prince of Balkh who renounced his kingdom and became a wandering ascetic. His life has often been compared to that of Buddha.

Allāh (Almighty and Glorious is He) saying: "O Ibrāhīm, say: 'O Allāh, make me content with Your judgment *[qaḍā']*, make me patient in the face of Your tribulation, and imbue me with gratitude for Your blessings. I beg You to grant the perfection of Your blessing, the permanence of Your gift of well-being, and the maintenance of Your love.'"

Our Prophet (Allāh bless him and give him peace) experienced a buzzing vibration *[ṭanīn]* in his heart. His heart withdrew from his people and he went out to Ḥirā, which is a section of Mount Sinai *[Ṭūr Sīnā']*. Along came the fragrant breeze of revelation *[waḥy]*. In it there was a cave, in which there was a worshipper *['ābid]* called Abū Kabsha. He came to his place to worship his Lord. While he was doing so, he saw a vision. The vision was like the break of dawn *[ṣubḥ]*. Then, when a voice cried: "O Muḥammad, O Muḥammad," he ran away from the voice and came back to his house, where he said: "Wrap me up, cover me with a blanket!"

I hear a voice. What is being said is: "O Muḥammad, this cannot be regulated by wrapping and covering with blankets."

> Allāh prevails in His purpose. (12:21)

This is the heart. It may be likened to a date stone in the courtyard of a house that has no roof, although it has four walls standing. The winter rain and the summer sun beat down upon it. The date plant grows, though no one sees it. When its tip eventually shows, as it shoots up tall, bears fruit and ripens, they come to gather from it but they have no access to the tree. So it is with the heart.

> Then, when He wills, He resurrects him. (80:22)

Saintship *[wilāya]* is an inner state *[bāṭina]*, carefully concealed. The foregoing analogy applies to saintship.

The angel is a confidential attendant *[farrāsh mubāṭan]* who is always in the immediate company of his Master, except when he goes off on an errand.

Do not ask anything of Allāh (Almighty and Glorious is He) apart from the assurance that you will have sufficient food, drink and clothing. Do not run away from Him. Do not worship Him for the sake of obtaining these things. What do you do with the mercy [of your Lord]?

Then the Shaikh (may Allāh the Exalted be well pleased with him) went on to say:

Make us independent of everyone but You. Do not keep us busy with anything other than You... What is this? (He wore a scowl of annoyance while saying this, then he covered his face and stood up shouting. Then he sat down, then stood up again and said:)

> And you will surely know the truth of it after a while. (38:88)

Some people are disinclined to ask for things from Allāh (Almighty and Glorious is He), in case this should result in their becoming greedy and ceasing to delegate their affairs and surrender their needs [to Him]. Ardent longing *[shawq]* is quickening their steps. When you are ready to abstain from the things of this world, it will be easy for you to give them away.

The saints *[awliyā']* of Allāh (Almighty and Glorious is He) have spiritual states *[aḥwāl]* that are peculiar to them. The *Badal* [spiritual deputy][10] does not become a *Badal* until all the burdens of his fellow creatures come to rest on his shoulders, although the Lord (Almighty and Glorious is He) relieves him of their weight, because he never leaves His presence. Outwardly it is he who carries the load, but inwardly the weight is supported by the hands of His mercy.

You need to acknowledge the truth when you hear it *['alaikum bi't-taṣdīq]* and to banish doubts from your hearts.

[10] *Badal* is the singular of *Abdāl.* In the Sixth Discourse of *Revelations of the Unseen,* Shaikh 'Abd al-Qādir (may Allāh be well pleased with him) gives the following explanation: "Annihilation *[fanā']* is the aim and object, the final destination of the journey of the saints. This was the direction sought by all previous saints and *Abdāl:* to become extinct to their own will, and let the will of the Almighty and Glorious Truth take its place, as a permanent transformation, lasting until death. That is why they came to be called *Abdāl* [lit: 'substitutes'] (may Allāh be well pleased with them all)." See also: *The Sublime Revelation,* p. 79.

The Shaikh (may Allāh be well pleased with him) also spoke about His words (Exalted is He):

> Keeping vigil by night is more potent in impact. (73:6)

This refers not only to giving up sleep in the ordinary sense, but also to giving up the sleep of involvement with creatures, the lower self *[nafs]*, natural inclination *[ṭab']*, passion *[hawā]* and willfulness *[irāda]*. For its food and drink the heart is left with speaking confidentially *[munājāt]* to Allāh (Almighty and Glorious is He), standing *[qiyām]* and bowing *[rukū']* and making prostration *[sujūd]* in His presence.

Surely you can see that if someone abstains from this world, so as not to be distracted by it from seeking the Lord of Truth (Almighty and Glorious is He), he must likewise abstain from the hereafter, so that it will not distract him from Allāh (Almighty and Glorious is He). He must wish that the hereafter did not exist, because it is so charming, such an obvious mercy. He must make the heart and the innermost being become a face, on the surface of which the contents of his heart are visible. He must want this world to last, because he is worshipping Allāh in secret, doing business with Him in secret.

You are in isolation from the Lord of Truth (Almighty and Glorious is He). When will you isolate your heart from creatures and seek the company of the Lord of Truth, going from door to door until there is no door left, from town to town, from heaven to heaven until there is no heaven left?

He [the believer] will bring the Resurrection upon himself. He will stand before the Lord of Truth (Almighty and Glorious is He), reading the records of his deeds, the good and the bad which consign him to the Fire [of Hell]. While he is caught between fear and hope, between falling into the Fire and crossing over it, Allāh (Exalted is He) will overtake him with His gracious kindness. He will put out the Fire with the water of His mercy, and the Fire will exclaim: "Pass through, O believer *[mu'min]*, since your light has extinguished my flames!" The passage—a journey that should take three thousand years—will be shortened for him to an instant, and then, when he is near to the palace of the King, he will recover his senses, his volition, his love for His Master *[Mawlā]* and his ardent longing for Him. He will say: "I shall not enter except in the company of the Beloved *[Maḥbūb]*."

Do you not see? [As we know from sayings of the Prophet (Allāh bless him and give him peace)], the miscarried fetus *[siqṭ]* will halt at the door of the Garden [of Paradise], saying: "I shall not enter until my parents enter. Where is the neighbor? Where is the witness?"

He will not enter until he is touched by the hand of the Prophet (Allāh bless him and give him peace) and he can go in to meet the Beloved. Then, when he has finally experienced this, he will be sent back into this world, in order to receive his full quota of the shares allotted by destiny *[aqsām]*, so that the [divine] foreknowledge *['ilm]* shall not be altered, abrogated and annulled. Your Lord has finished with the work of creation.

[As the Prophet (Allāh bless him and give him peace) has said:]

> No soul shall depart from this world until it has received its allotted share *[qism]* in full.

You must therefore be dutifully devoted to Allāh (Almighty and Glorious is He) and have the decency to look to the Lord of Truth for what you need, instead of to His creatures. The material means *[asbāb]* are a screen.

The King's doors are locked. If you turn away from them, there will be opened unto you a door you can recognize. The door of the innermost being has swung shut *[bābu's-sirri sāra ilā sadd]*, but then it is opened without your own power and strength.

The believer *[mu'min]* must leave his natural inclination *[ṭab']* behind, moving in the direction of his Lord. As long as he is following this present course, he is exposed to harmful influences affecting his person and his property. He is reverting to his sins, to his bad behavior and to infringing the rules *[ḥudūd]* of the sacred law *[shar']* of his Lord. He must not seek help through supplication *[du'ā']*, nor must he seek help from anyone other than his Lord. No, he must remember his sins and practice self-criticism until, when he has done a thorough job of this, he can resort to acceptance of the decree of destiny *[qadar]*, to surrender *[taslīm]* and entrustment *[tafwīḍ]* as far as his heart is concerned. Once he is in this state, he will see an open door.

> Whoever is dutiful toward Allāh, He prepares a way out for him. (65:2)

He puts His servant to the test to see how he will behave:

> And We have put them to the test with good things and bad things. (7:168)

The heart of the son of Adam must continue to travel along the path of good and evil, honor and humiliation, wealth and poverty, until he finally acknowledges that all blessings are due to Allāh (Almighty and Glorious is He). This means gratitude *[shukr]*—and gratitude is an act of obedience *[ṭāʿa]* performed without moving the tongue and the limbs of the body—and patient endurance of misfortune. He must admit his sins and offenses until, having taken his last step on the good side and his last step on the bad side, there he is at the King's door. He has taken the step of gratitude and the step of patience, with divine help *[tawfīq]* as the guide. He has seen the King's door, and beyond it he can see things that no eye ever saw, that no ear ever heard of, and that never occurred to any human heart. The alternating sequence of good moves and bad moves is at an end; now comes the turn of conversation, discourse and sitting in company [with the Lord].

Can you grasp this, O ʿIraqī, O camel at the mill, O stupid fool? You go through the motions of ritual prayer *[anta fī qiyām wa-quʿūd]* without sincerity. You perform the prayers *[tuṣallī]* for the sake of other people, and while you are fasting *[taṣūmu]* your eyes are on their dishes of food and on the contents of their houses.

O alien to the human race, O straggler from the ranks of the champions of truth *[ṣiddīqūn]* and the Lord's own people *[rabbāniyyūn]*! Do you not realize that I am your goldsmith's furnace, your probe and your touchstone? Do your utmost. Refuse to let me eat from your plate. Unsheathe your sword against me. You do not amount to anything. O little ignoramus, I am twisting your reins. I am giving you good advice and treating you with compassion. I am afraid that you may die an atheist *[zindīq]*, a pretender *[murā'ī]*, an impostor *[dajjāl]*—doomed to suffer in your grave the punishment of the hypocrites *[munāfiqūn]*. So you must desist from what you are up to. You must strip yourself naked and then put on the clothes of dutiful devotion *[taqwā]*. You will soon be dead. There is no hostility between me and you. You will have cause to remember what I am saying to you.

The insight of the righteous man *[ṣāliḥ]* is indicative of his spiritual state *[ḥāl]*. When someone really knows *['arafa]* Allāh, his tongue falls silent; he is free from want because of Him, and of Him alone he is in need.

In my childhood, back in my home town, I used to hear someone saying to me, "O blessed one *[yā mubārak]*." I would run away from that voice, but then in solitude I would hear someone saying to me: "I think well of you."

If you wish for success *[falāḥ]* you must stick close to me. When you see a person running away from me, you must know that he is a hypocrite.

The believer *[mu'min]* is such that, when he closes the eyes in his head, the eyes of his heart are opened and he sees what is over there; and when he closes the eyes of his heart, the eyes in his head are opened and he sees the situation of Allāh and His dealings with His creatures.

The words of Allāh addressed to Moses (peace be upon him) include the following:

> I have chosen you above all men to receive My mission and My words. (7:144)

"And I have drawn you close to Me. One day you were shepherding a flock of sheep when one of them strayed off, so you followed after it until you caught up with it. By then you were exhausted, as it was exhausted, so you picked it up and hugged it and you said: 'You have worn yourself out and you have worn me out.'"

The remedy for someone who is separated [from the Lord] is detecting the cause of his separation, turning from it in repentance and confessing it in His presence.

The sinless ones *[ma'ṣūmūn]*, those who are protected from every aspect, they do not have creative power *[takwīn]*. Creative power comes in the process of following the path *[fi'ṭ-ṭarīq]*. There is nothing worth talking about until you cross the wastelands, the deserts, the two continents and the two oceans —the continent of creatures and the continent of the self *[nafs]*, the ocean of the law *[ḥukm]* and the ocean of knowledge *['ilm]*—as well as the shore.

For the people [of the Lord] there is neither night nor day. Their diet is the diet of the sick and their sleep is the sleep of the drowned. Their speech is only out of necessity. When someone really knows Allāh, his tongue falls silent, but "when He wills, He resurrects him" (80:22), and then he speaks without instruments, without tools, without preparation, without time for thought, without pretext. There is no difference between his tongue and his finger. Thus there is no wall of separation, no restriction, no door and no doorman, no permission to be granted or sought, no authorization and no dismissal, no Satan and no sultan, no inner core *[janān]* and no fingertips *[banān]*.

Then the Shaikh (may Allāh the Exalted be well pleased with him) said:

A loser is he who is absent today. You do not take the first step, and the second cannot be taken. The first is leaving the house of your worldly existence *[wujūd]*, and the second is His blessing:

> Praise be to Allāh, Lord of All the Worlds. (1:1)

—while standing at the door:

> You alone do we worship, and of You alone do we seek help. (1:5)

—and when beholding Him:

> And prostrate yourself and draw near. (96:19)

After the vision of Him, blessings cannot be attributed to anyone other than Him. You are are attributing partners to Him *[mushrik]*. You are altering the blessings of Allāh. Allāh may change whatever blessing you yourself enjoy. Cut the cord *[zunnār]* and come back! Your outer *[ẓāhir]* is of no importance until your inner *[bāṭin]* repents and center of your being *[sarīra]* is devoted to your Lord.

O young man, O dear young man! When Prophethood came to the Prophet (Allāh bless him and give him peace), he kept it a secret for several years. He digested it bit by bit, until he was told:

> Make known that which has been sent down to you from your Lord. (5:67)

When you experience something, however, you make it public and do not keep it hidden. You happened to receive a bale of clothes from your home, so you opened your door and called out: "Come, buy from me!" Perhaps it was meant to be a loan, or a deposit to be held in trust on behalf of the neighbors.

Four things are conducive to soundness of the heart. The first is checking to make sure one has something fit to eat. The second is undisturbed devotion to worshipful obedience *[ṭā'a]*. The third is the preservation of honorable dignity. The fourth is giving up everything that distracts you from Allāh.

As for checking to make sure you have a morsel fit to eat, this is something about which you simply do not have a clue. This matter can only be dealt with correctly by means of healthy restraint *[wara' shāfī]*, and by pausing in His presence and imploring Him to keep one's religion *[dīn]* safe. The believer *[mu'min]* must pause before taking anything to eat or drink, seeking permission from the Book and the Sunna, until he draws close to his Master (Almighty and Glorious is He). Then he will carry out His commandment and observe His prohibition, knowing through His knowledge *['ilm]* and helped by His support.

You must renew the covenant *['ahd]* with Him before death. You will see clearly when the dust has settled, O seekers, O ignorant ones, O heedless ones!

And you will surely know the truth of it after a while. (38:88)

Question: The lower self *[nafs]* is so treacherous; how can I accept its verdict [*fatwā:* opinion on a point of Islamic law]?

To this the Shaikh replied:

You must struggle against it until it dies, then bring it back to a new life, resurrected as a qualified jurist *[faqīha]*, a learned scholar *['ālima]*, calm and tranquil *[muṭmainna]*. You must lock the door of its carnal appetites and pleasures. Keep it from having access to its carnal desires *[shahawāt]* until, when it has withered away, its desires return to your innermost being *[sirr]*. It will be transformed into a heart *[qalb]* through dedicated struggle *[mujāhada]*.

The people [of the Lord] look forward eagerly to the coming of night and the time when their dependants have gone to sleep, because they have many obligations. They must carry the burdens of their dependants and their material means *[asbāb]*. Although their hearts are in a state of calm reliance on their Lord (Almighty and Glorious is He), their physical limbs and organs are actively engaged in dealing with the material means.

If you have been dutifully devoted *[muttaqī]* before being put to the test, you will not resort during the time of tribulation to anyone but Him. You will not expect anyone but Him to provide relief from it. You will regard both the good and the bad as having their source in His presence, along with harm and benefit, honor and humiliation, affluence and poverty.

Question: What is meant by the saying of a certain righteous man: "If a glance *[laḥza]* does nothing useful for you, a sermon *[wa'ẓa]* will do you no good."

The Shaikh (may Allāh be well pleased with him) said in reply:

There are people from whose eyes and hearts both this world and the hereafter have vanished away, and who have seen their Lord, so if they glance at you they bring you benefit. If the saint *[walī]* looks at parched earth, Allāh will revive it and cause it to put forth vegetation, or if he looks at a Jew *[Yahūdī]* or a Christian *[Naṣrānī]*, Allāh will guide them aright.

Someone said to him: "Why do we see you hugging this piece of wood, the pommel *[rummāna]* of the lectern *[kursī]*?" So he said:

Because it is close to me. You see things but do not report them or point them out, so that is why I embrace them.

The person said to him: "So we are nearer to your heart?" He replied:

O my foster-brother[11], you will be like that only when you are all dutifully devoted to Allāh (Exalted is He), when you are vigilantly aware of Him, fear Him and seek Him. In me you will have a servant and a loving friend.

If the servant leads an ascetic life, getting steadily weaker and more and more emaciated, Allāh will open the door for him, draw him near and bring him close. Overlooking his failure to acquire knowledge *['ilm]*, He will show him what knowledge is and will teach it to him. To live in obscurity, poorly nourished and emaciated, is one form of proper conduct *[ḥusn al-adab]*.

[11] Literally, "son of my wet nurse *[ibn dāyatī]*." Relationships established through fosterage have considerable importance in Islamic law. For instance, intermarriage between milk-relatives is forbidden, as it is between blood-relatives.

The people [of the Lord] give expression, with their physical organs, their hearts, their secret souls *[sarāʾir]* and their inner recesses *[khalawāt]*, to the noble attributes *[makārim]* of their Lord. They have become dutifully devoted servants *[atqiyāʾ]*. They have become noblemen in His sight.

For one of you, the object of worship *[maʿbūd]* is his dirham [silver coin] and his dīnār [gold coin]. If he lost his money, it would be the end of the world as far as he is concerned, yet when he misses a Friday prayer or some other congregational prayer *[ṣalāt jumʿa aw jamāʿa]*, it does not bother him at all. Or if an immoral, dissolute son of his should die on him, his distress would be very great and he would seek comfort with one of his fellow creatures, rather than turning for consolation to the angels who are by his side. When the servant's heart is pure, he is on intimate terms with the angels, and they will often speak to him in private.

O exile from the Lord of Truth, O exile from the sacred law *[sharʿ]* and religion *[dīn]*! O resident of this world, attached to the lower self *[nafs]* and natural inclinations *[ṭabʿ]*! O worshipper of creatures *[khalq]*, O forgetter of the Truth *[Ḥaqq]*! There is no way of avoiding the encounter with Allāh (Exalted is He). Meet Him now! Leave creatures and the lower self behind, then you will meet the Lord of Truth. Apart from remembrance *[dhikr]* of Him, all is in vain. Apart from knowledge *[ʿilm]* of Him, all is in vain. All dealings with others apart from Him must end in failure.

Seekers of this world are many, but seekers of the hereafter are few, and few indeed are those who seek the Lord of Truth (Almighty and Glorious is He). You are caught up with this world of yours by night and day. It uses you and cuts you off. We make use of it and everything that operates within it. So how about you, O backslider? There is no way of coping with it without the help of the sacred law *[sharʿ]* and knowledge *[ʿilm]*. You must accept whatever advice they offer you, and from everything which they advise against you must refrain.

You do not know how to engage in intimate conversation *[tanājī]* with your Lord. You must pause in the midst of your buying and selling, your eating, your taking and giving and your talking.

Whatever belongs to Allāh, take full advantage of it, and whatever belongs to anyone other than Him, have nothing to do with it.

When love has a person under its control, he ceases to distinguish between this world and the hereafter, between giving and withholding, between acceptance and rejection. His heart is filled with His love. The good and the bad sides of his Beloved are merged as one, and the doors and avenues to Him are all combined. Love lumps all that together. Hearsay and direct evidence become one and the same, as do injury and benefit. His heart is always in ecstasy *[wajd]*. Sometimes what he experiences through the remembrance *[dhikr]* of Allāh (Exalted is He) is a taste of Divine Majesty *[jalāl]*, while at other times the remembrance of Allāh will give him an experience of Divine Beauty *[jamāl]*. His daylight is perplexing; the closer he gets to it, the more remote it becomes, just like the fire of Moses (peace be upon him). Whenever he approached it, it would move away, until he finally heard the voice crying:

> I am indeed Allāh. (28:30)

The heart goes through a similar experience. It sees the radiant lights of nearness [to the Lord], and whenever it advances toward them they move further away:

> Until the prescribed term is fulfilled. (2:235)

When no more steps are taken, the prescribed term is fulfilled. The situation is turned around. The seeker *[ṭālib]* becomes one who is sought *[maṭlūb]*, the pursuer *[qāṣid]* one who is pursued *[maqṣūd]*, the wisher *[murīd]* one who is wished for *[murād]*.

Just one pull of the attraction *[jadhba]* exerted by the Lord of Truth is better than all the work of men and jinn *['amal ath-thaqalain]*.

He sees His servant leaving the house of his natural inclinations *[ṭab']*, his carnal desires *[shahawāt]* and his passions *[hawā]*, saying goodbye to creatures, giving up his carnal desires, going in search of Him, experiencing a transformation; he is in a state of restless agitation, with no provisions for the journey, no beast to ride and no traveling companion; he spends both night and day in fasting *[ṣiyām]*, prayer *[ṣalāt]* and dedicated struggle *[mujāhada]*. While he is in this condition, he suddenly finds that he is at the door of His nearness, in the bosom of His grace, at the table of His bountiful favor, witnessing his own preordained destiny *[sābiqa]*.

You aspire to the heights, but you are stuck in the mud. You aspire to the Garden [of Paradise], but you are not doing the work that must be done in order to gain entry to it.

A certain righteous man once said: "You must restrain your lower self *[nafs]* from its familiar habits. Do not eat just because it is the natural thing to do. You must not take a single morsel without specific authorization from Allāh (Exalted is He), nor must you take any medicine except on His prescription, for His ingredients may be the opposite of what comes out of the medical handbooks and what the doctors would recommend."

> And He takes good care of the righteous. (7:196)

His physician is the Beloved, who takes care of him at home and decides what he should have to eat and drink.

Then the Shaikh uttered a tremendous cry, stood up and started swaying, sometimes to his right and sometimes to his left, as he raised his hands heavenward in a gesture of submission *[taslīm]*. He went on like this till the end of his session *[majlis]*, then he cried: "Oh, what a blazing inferno! Oh, what a disaster for you all!" Then he held out his hands in supplication. He sat down to offer the prayer of supplication *[du'ā']* without speaking. Then, when he stood up again, his face kept changing color, sometimes turning pale yellow and sometimes appearing bright red.

When the heart transcends this world and becomes the guest of the nearness of the Lord of Truth (Almighty and Glorious is He), it refuses to accept any kind of dependence on creatures. From the Throne *[ʿarsh]* on high to the earth below, it is as if creatures had never been created, as if Allāh had never brought anything into being, as if He had never created anyone but him, meaning the owner of this heart that is being described. One belongs to One *[wāḥid li-wāḥid]*, lover *[muḥibb]* and Beloved *[maḥbūb]*, seeker *[ṭālib]* and Sought *[maṭlūb]*, he who remembers *[dhākir]* and He who is remembered *[madhkūr]*; he can see no one but Him.

The Shaikh (may Allāh the Exalted be well pleased with him) also said:

The news has come to me about the kind of calamity that will befall this city [of Baghdād].

Then he offered a supplication on behalf of the inhabitants of the city, praying that they be spared. Then he said, like someone who is feeling dejected:

By my life, there is indeed someone in this city who deserves to be killed and crucified. For one individual whom You honor, however, there are a thousand individuals on account of whom You will destroy us; You will make us suffer for their sins. What have we done? (He says this with a note of exasperation.) You have put friend and foe into the furnace of destiny *[qadar]* and they have both melted down and become a single ingot.

Do not look for anything in the way of charismatic gifts *[karāmāt]* and miracles *[muʿjizāt]*. Do not try to compete with Prophets when it comes to miracles, nor with the saints *[awliyāʾ]* where charismatic gifts are concerned, if you wish for the nearness of the Lord of Truth and His fellowship. Once that fellowship is here to stay, He will feed and you will have something to eat, He will clothe you and you will have something to wear. To desire these things is an obstacle, and to reject them after their arrival is also an obstacle.

When the saints *[awliyāʾ]* are being brought along the road to the

Lord of Truth (Almighty and Glorious is He), they are served by the jinn, by human beings and by the angels. They glean wherever they alight *[ainamā saqaṭū laqaṭū]*, until they reach Him. The heat of this world and of physical existence *[wujūd]* eventually leaves them. Beyond this point they are attended by grace and tender care until, when He grants them permission to enter the door of nearness, they are smitten with afflictions, the afflictions of Divine Majesty *[jalāl]*, so that their lower selves *[nufūs]* get dissolved, along with any remnants of their worldly existence. All means of support for the outer *[ẓāhir]* are withheld: the food of the outer, its clothing and everything that keeps it fit and well. The heart is left naked, together with the pure innermost being *[sirr]*. They are now presented with the food of bountiful favor, the wine of intimate friendship *[uns]*, the crown of honor, the garments of good will. They are offered morsel after morsel of mystic knowledge *['ilm ladunī]* and wisdom *[ḥikma]*, then the King lets them know their names *[asmā']*. He makes known to them the blessings bestowed in the past, in bygone ages. He makes them thoroughly familiar with all this before He returns them to ordinary existence, for the sake of improving them and equipping them to provide right guidance *[hidāya]* and direction *[dalāla]* and to function as mediators *[sifāra]*. Then He empowers their hearts with creative force *[takwīn]*, and their tongues with the ability not only to make requests and supplications but also to receive answers.

This is the end of the age, the era of hypocrisy *[nifāq]*. Vanity *['ujb]* is rampant; unbelief *[kufr]* is rampant and presents an obstacle [to spiritual progress]. Vanity causes you to lose the respect of the Lord (Almighty and Glorious is He). Both of them are repugnant; both obstruct access to the path *[ṭarīq]*.

If anyone should ask: "What is hypocrisy, so that we can avoid it?" tell him that the Prophet (Allāh bless him and give him peace) has said:

> The hypocrite? When he makes a promise, he breaks it; when he tells you something, he is lying; and when he is trusted, he cheats.

The believer *[mu'min]* has no clothes, no food, no marriage, no happiness, no security and no fixed abode, until he sees the place where he belongs and hears his title *[laqab]*; until he sees his preordainment *[sābiqa]* and his proper name *[ism]* in his solitary retreat. He wanders through the wastelands and deserts, placing his trust in destiny *[qadar]*, and the angels *[malā'ika]* notice his condition and hear his title. "Who is this?" the angels ask, then they tell one another, "This is dear so and so, the beloved champion of the truth *[aṣ-ṣiddīq]*, one of forty, or of seven, or of three. He owns such and such." Destiny maneuvers him to right and left. Destiny controls his movements and supplies him with food.

> And Allāh, all unseen, surrounds them. (85:20)

He hears the words from a voice near his heart, saying: "Go back to your home. Look after your treasure. Keep yourself out of sight. Pretend it was all a dream, a flight experienced by your heart and your innermost being."

You must stick to the book of the law *[ḥukm]* and then to the book of knowledge *['ilm]*, until you reach maturity and your youth is past and gone. Only then will He clothe you and feed you. You want to have this now, when you are still full of natural urges *[ṭab']*, passions *[hawā]* and carnal desires *[shahwa]*. Even when you stand ready to perform the prayer *[ṣalāt]*, you are actually buying and selling, eating, drinking and engaging in sexual activity with your heart, because of your susceptibility to temptation *[waswasa]*.

Someone asked the Shaikh (May Allāh the Exalted be well pleased with him): "What is the remedy for this?" and he replied:

[First of all,] making sure that what you eat is pure and uncontaminated by anything unlawful *[ḥarām]* or dubious *[shubha]*. The second remedy is to refuse to let the lower self *[nafs]* have its way, whenever it tries to make you do something that is forbidden.

If the servant is disturbed by a statement *[kalima]* that is suddenly inspired in his heart, and he gets into a state of agitation, another will be added to it. His agitation will then diminish and his disturbance will dissipate, and yet another will be added. As a calm and quiet state is reached, his agitation will depart completely.

He will be addressed by all and sundry [*al-ḥajar wa'l-madar:* desert dwellers and city dwellers] as he follows his path, providing confirmation and reassurance. People will say to him, "O saint *[walī]* of Allāh! O you who are sought after *[murād]* by Allāh! O friend *[ḥabīb]* of His! O you who have been drawn near *[muqarrab]* to Him!"

A man said to him: "Pray for me *[ud'u lī],*" so the Shaikh (may Allāh be well pleased with him) replied:

O Allāh, let me find all I need in You, to the exclusion of all creatures, and let him find all he needs in remembrance of You, without having to ask.

When someone no longer has any need of creatures, he clings to the door of the Lord of Truth (Almighty and Glorious is He), who then enriches him with His nearness. When He has enriched him with His nearness, he becomes too preoccupied with remembering Him and thanking Him to consider asking Him for anything.

When you are deprived of food and water out in the deserts, a fountain will gush forth for you in your own home.

Creatures are the most powerful weapon Satan has against you.

Beautify your heart, then your external appearance *[ẓāhir].*

The distraction, the whole distraction, resides in the abode of creatures and their dwelling place.

A worthy lover goes forth in search of his beloved. Joseph (peace be upon him) went forth in search of Jacob. Anyone who set eyes on him found him attractive and fell passionately in love with him. He took to wearing a veil, but he was thrown in prison. His only goal was Jacob, none of the others. [In the words of the poet:]

Would that all between me and thee might flourish,
and all between me and the rest of the world might lie in ruins!

The crier of the Lord of Truth has come. Abandon the building of creatures:

> Until the prescribed term is fulfilled. (2:235)

There is nothing worth talking about until the water has drained away from your frog *[ḍifdaʿ]*. Until the dry land is clear for His worship, your innermost being *[sirr]* is with Him aboard the ship of His power *[qudra]*. As He told him [Noah] by inspiration:

> In the Name of Allāh shall be its course and its mooring (11:41)

—in the ocean of knowledge *['ilm]*.

Being in the company of the servants of Allāh is like being in the company of a lion; fear and wariness are appropriate in both cases. As long as the lion has something else to keep him satisfied, he will not concern himself with you, because all his attention is directed elsewhere, but if you go and bother him instead of retiring to a safe distance, he will savage you. To be in the company of the champion of truth *[ṣiddīq]* is much the same, because that is how they are in the company of the King.

Among the companions of al-Junaid there was a man who was having doubts about the spontaneously arising notion *[khāṭir]*. Al-Junaid was made aware of this, so he asked the man: "What they are saying about you, is it true?" He said, "Yes," [so al-Junaid said:] "Let an utterance come through your heart." The man said, "Very well," and when asked what he had uttered [inwardly], he replied: "I uttered such and such." But [al-Junaid] said: "No, [that wasn't it]!" Then the man tried again, and when he reported [what he had uttered inwardly], he was again told: "No!" He then let one more utterance come to him through his heart, and reported to al-Junaid, who yet again said: "No!" So the man said: "O Shaikh, my experience is genuine, so you had better check your own!" To this al-Junaid replied: "I knew that everything you told me was true. I simply wanted to test the purity of your heart and its steadfastness."[*]

Their hearts [the hearts of the people of the Lord] are the channels of His will *[irāda]*, the treasure houses of His knowledge *['ilm]*, the bosom of His mystery *[sirr]*, the treasure houses of destiny in the Valley of Destiny *[wādī'l-qadar]*. Whenever their innermost beings *[asrār]* go on a tour within the precincts of the palace of destiny, they become acquainted with all kinds of knowledge *['ulūm]* and secrets *[asrār]*.

What can be built with well-propped timber! What can be made of outer forms *[ṣuwar]* with no inner content *[ma'nā]*?

> Deaf, dumb, blind, so they do not understand. (2:171)

A certain person wrote three hundred and sixty stories, delivering one story every day to the local prince *[amīr]*. He never got too bored to keep trying, until at long last he received the official seal of approval he was seeking to obtain. In your case, however, you devote a few short days or a few short nights to making requests of Allāh (Exalted is He), then you get bored and resort to creatures instead. Why not remember the man who wrote all those stories?

As long as you remain attached to creatures, you will not prosper. You must turn in repentance from creatures to the Lord of Truth, and let your standing in waiting be at the threshold of the door of His nearness. The hand of love and nearness will draw you in. You will come to be a permanent fixture *[ḥils]* of that mansion. Eventually, as you experience all the facilities and amenities, comfort will come to you from every side. Your wing will grow strong and you will fly up to the battlements of that mansion. Those battlements will come to be your tower. If you fall, you will fall into the palace courtyard. You will spend all your time in the presence of the Owner of the palace. You will be a petitioner whose requests are granted.

If you wish to promote the welfare of your fellow creatures, this is how you must go about it, instead of spouting useless drivel. (The Shaikh—may Allāh be well pleased with him—was getting at the sermons delivered to the people by the preachers *[wu''āẓ]*.)

To perform the prayer *[ṣalāt]* is to make a connection *[ṣila]* with Allāh (Exalted is He) after becoming detached from everything other than Him. The body cannot be divided up between two situations, detachment *[infiṣāl]* from creatures and attachment *[ittiṣāl]* to the Lord of Truth. This refers to the prayer of the people [of the Lord]. As for the prayer of ordinary servants *['ibād]*, the way they go about it is to set the Garden [of Paradise] to the right of the heart, the Fire [of Hell] to the left of it, and the Narrow Bridge *[ṣirāṭ]* in front of it, with the Lord watching over it. As for the prayer of the lovers *[muḥibbūn]*, it is detachment from creatures and attachment to Him.

The sure sign that your lower self *[nafs]* is genuinely in need of food is that you hear something crying from your inner *[bāṭin]*, like the sound made by young chickens. When you hear that sound, you must provide it with what it needs for its survival.

As Allāh (Exalted is He) has said:

> And He has inspired it [the self] with what is wrong for it and what is right for it. (91:8)
>
> It is He who makes us laugh and makes us weep. (53:43)

You cannot put these two verses of the Qur'ān into practice until after the heart has entered the presence of its King. It is only then that the action and the inspiration come about. Before the entry has been made, you must distinguish between a direct inner receiving *[wārid fī bāṭinika]* and a suggestion inspired *[ilhām]* by the devil *[shaiṭān]*, by a natural impulse *[ṭab']*, by a selfish instinct *[nafs]*, or by an angel *[malak]*.

If you wish to join someone's company for the sake of pleasing Allāh (Almighty and Glorious is He), you must perform your minor ablution *[wuḍū']* with meticulous correctness, while the mind is inactive and the eyes are not wandering. Then proceed to perform your prayer *[ṣalāt]*. You will open the door of the prayer with your ritual purity *[ṭuhūr]*, and the door of your Lord with your prayer. Then ask Him, when you have finished: "Whom should I take as a guide *[dalīl]*? Who is the one who can report on Your authority? Who is the one singled out *[mufrad]*? Who is the deputy *[khalīfa]*? Who is the delegate *[nā'ib]*?" He is Generous *[Karīm]*, He will not let you suffer disappointment. Without a doubt, He will grant inspiration *[yulhimu]* to your heart. He will grant revelation *[yūḥī]* to your innermost being *[sirr]*. He will show you a clear sign. He will open the doors to shed light on your path. Someone who seeks and strives will surely find *[man ṭalaba wa-jadda wajada]*.

> As for those who strive in Our cause, surely We shall guide them to Our paths. (29:69)

The decisive factor lies within you, not in what he [someone you are thinking of joining] has to say, so when all the angles have converged from your heart's point of view, and everything points to a particular individual, go ahead and join his company. Your fellowship with him should be for you like the fellowship of lions and snakes. Pay no attention to his poverty, the gaps in his pedigree, his straitened circumstances, his shabby appearance and his clumsy mode of expression. What is really significant *[al-ma'nā]* about him resides in his inner being *[bāṭin]*, not in his outer *[ẓāhir]*, not in his physical constitution and not on his face.

Do not be in a hurry to speak, and do not try to get his attention straight away. Be on the lookout for the useful service he performs on behalf of his Lord. He is the clerk, and the instructions he notes down are not for himself but for others. He is an ambassador. He is the waiter, and the dish is for someone else. He is the communicator, and the communication is for someone other than himself. You must therefore be ready to receive what Allāh may disclose by means of his tongue. Do not wander out of his sight. Do not overstep his limit, but always stand waiting with head bowed in silence, fearful and timid. Do not harbor doubts concerning his spiritual state *[ḥāl]*, nor about his words and his actions. You must consider him superior to any clever person, and let him steer you from his presence toward his Lord, not toward any other.

The joker you should not encourage. The prattler you should not respond to.

We have been given the same natural disposition as the animals, but the intellect *['aql]* discriminates, the sacred law *[shar']* discriminates, knowledge *['ilm]* discriminates, nearness *[qurb]* discriminates, direct experience *[ma'rifa]* and obedient service *[ṭā'a]* discriminate, while the original source is One.

If they put their knowledge into practice, when they came across a dead man they would bring him back to life, or in the case of a sinner they would remind him to mend his ways.

Bowls are brought to him in his house, for other people. He proceeds to collect the tax *[kharāj]* and then, when he has collected it, he hands it over to the King. He also has a salary *[jāmikiyya]*. He takes from the people, but not for himself.

When Allāh wishes you well, He wakes you up and makes you aware of your own faults.

Your learned scholar *['ālim]* is an ignorant man. Your ignorant man is a slanderous liar. Your pious abstainer *[zāhid]* is full of worldly desires.

Do not exploit your religion *[dīn]* for worldly gain. Only the hereafter can be gained through religion.

The Shaikh (may Allāh the Exalted be well pleased with him) also spoke about His words (Exalted is He):

> Call upon your Lord humbly and in secret; He does not love those who go too far in the wrong direction *[al-mu'tadīn]*. (7:55)

He gave this verse of the Qur'ān its literal interpretation, since in this context the obvious meaning of *al-mu'tadī* [singular of *al-mu'tadīn,* which sometimes means 'aggressors'] is a person who calls upon anyone other than Him, one who puts his requests to anyone apart from Him.

'Abdullāh ibn Mas'ūd[12] used to say to his companions: "You are the polish *[jilā']* of my heart." If a person is ready to listen to me for the sake of Allāh and for the benefit to be derived from my

[12] Abū 'Abd ar-Raḥmān 'Abdullāh ibn Mas'ūd al-Hudhalī (d. A.H. 32 or 33). One of the earliest and closest Companions of the Prophet (Allāh bless him and give him peace). A man of lowly antecedents, he became an authority on the recitation and interpretation of the Qur'ān, as well as an expert on Islamic law and the Prophetic tradition.

words, he will be a kind of polish, but otherwise he should stay away from me, for his presence will cast a cloud.

When Abraham (peace be upon him) had escaped from the fiery furnace, and his livestock and servants had come to be many, he had a mansion built in Syria, with numerous entrances. He retired to live there after he had paid off the cost of construction, and said farewell to his people. He went into retirement in order to provide training for his successors *[khalaf]*.

What is "bosom friendship" *[khulla]* ?[13] It is companionship *[ṣuḥba]*, loving affection *[maḥabba]* and togetherness *[wuṣla]*.

Question: Should one follow the verbal teaching *[qāl]* of the guide, or his spiritual state *[ḥāl]*?

The Shaikh (may Allāh be well pleased with him) responded to this by saying:

The verbal teaching is what the common people *['awāmm]* follow, while the spritual state is emulated by the special few *[khawāṣṣ]*. Which group do you belong to? Let me feel your pulse, so I can diagnose your condition, show you how serious your sickness is, and cure you. The regular practice of our Prophet (Allāh bless him and give him peace) included visiting the sick. We have been prevented from doing that, but we do visit the healthy with our spiritual influence *[himma]*. Our legs have been prevented from walking to your houses, and our hands from taking your property. We have been so commanded by virtue of the spiritual state *[ḥāl]* and the decree of destiny *[qadar]*

[13] The Prophet Abraham (peace be upon him) is called *Khalīlu'llāh*, the 'Bosom Friend' of Allāh. The abstract noun *khulla* is formed from the same Arabic 'root' — *kh-l-l* — as *khalīl*.

The Shaikh (may Allāh, Exalted is He, be well pleased with him) also said:

Suppose that a certain man is about to die, leaving ten sons to succeed him, all of them on the same level in terms of dutiful devotion to their father. [According to the Islamic law of inheritance], they would each be entitled to an equal share in his estate, but the father's heart is inclined toward one son in particular, and he wishes that he could inherit the whole of his estate. Then along comes destiny with the decree of death for one son after another, until only that favored one is left alive. He comes into possession of the whole of his father's estate, since the judgment *[qaḍā']* and decree of destiny *[qadar]* have taken effect. Is there anything wrong in this? Let us leave it there for now *[ilā hāhunā wa's-salām]*.

O Allāh, keep creatures at a distance from us. Keep the lower self *[nafs]* at a distance from us, as well as the passions *[ahwiya]* and natural urges *[ṭibā']*.

You said, "I am afraid of this ocean," yet you are swimming in it, which would indicate the very opposite of being afraid.

> Only those of His servants fear Allāh who have knowledge. (38:28)

Once they have come to know, they become afraid. You have come to know how harmful the thing is, so be on your guard against it and avoid it. Death will come to you inevitably, so work to be ready for it. O you whose house is without a roof, whose dependants have no flour to make bread, no underclothes to wear and no blankets to cover them! The winter is coming, so be prepared. The commander *[amīr]* is coming, so get down off your high horse. The lion is coming, so beware of the lion of death.

What is the meaning of those words you pronounce while performing your prayer *[ṣalāt]*?

> You alone do we worship *[iyyāka na'budu]*, and of You alone do we seek help *[wa-iyyāka nasta'īn]*. (1:5)

[They mean:] "You alone do we obey *[iyyāka nuṭī'u]*, and You alone do we acknowledge as the One God *[wa-iyyāka nuwaḥḥidu]*."

When have you ever affirmed the Oneness of the Lord of Truth (Almighty and Glorious is He)? When have you ever done anything with true sincerity? When have you ever abstained from creatures, from pretense *[riyā']* and hypocrisy *[nifāq]* and rowdy contention *[ṣakhab]*? When have you ever submitted humbly to the Lord of Truth, with the kind of humility that is experienced in the heart, in private?

If the carnal desire of the lower self *[nafs]* interferes with someone's vision of the Lord of Truth, he will feel too ashamed to behold Him, so he must get rid of that lustful desire. When will you see Jacob (peace be upon him) biting the tips of his fingers, in your own private space, when your lust *[shabaq]* is intense? When will you realize what keeps you chaste? That which preserves your chastity *['iṣma]* is the jealousy *[ghaira]* of Allāh (Almighty and Glorious is He). When Joseph (peace be upon him) met that woman, the divine jealousy intervened, so he turned and ran away.

> So it was, that We might ward off from him evil and lewdness; he was one of Our devoted servants. (12:24)

When will your condition be transformed into that of Joseph (peace be upon him)? When Joseph (peace be upon him) was made responsible for preserving chastity in the House of Allāh and its sacred precincts, he complied with the will of his Lord in his confinement, and He bestowed chastity upon him in his seclusion. This is how you must be, O servants of Allāh, O seekers! Borrow the condition of the champion of truth *[ṣiddīq]*. Ask for it from Allāh!

Absolute trust *[tawakkul]* means cutting off all material means *[asbāb]*, letting everything go. When the servant's heart *[qalb]* is transformed *[inqalaba]*, it will become an angel *[malak]*. He will hear what the angel hears. He will experience what the angel experiences. Then it will develop even further, so that it becomes a king *[malik]* ruling over him.

The Shaikh (may Allāh be well pleased with him) also said, concerning the story of Moses (peace be upon him):

The innermost being *[sirr]* is the secret of the mystery *[sirru's-sirr]*. He left his family when he noticed a fire in the direction of the mountain. What did he see? The eye of the head saw a fire *[nār]*, while the eye of the heart saw a light *[nūr]*. The eye of the head saw a creation *[khalqan]*, while the eye of the heart saw a Divine Truth *[ḥaqqan]*.

> He said to his household: "Stay here awhile, I notice a fire." (28:29)

It attracted him through his heart, and disposed him to relinquish control of his wife and his children.

"He said to his household, 'Stay here awhile...'" A summons has come from on high. The grappling irons of destiny have snatched the people [of the Lord] away from their wives and their children. O law *[ḥukm]*, stay in place! O knowledge *['ilm]*, advance in the name of Allāh! O lower self *[nafs]*, stay in place! O heart *[qalb]* and innermost being *[sirr]*, respond! What a loser is he who fails to grasp this, who does not love this, who does not believe in this! How great his loss, how great his loss! How far apart he must remain! How terrrible for him!

> Perhaps I shall bring you news of it. (28:29)

"Stay there where you are, until I bring you news of the path." Because he had in fact strayed from the path. Its signposts were out of his sight. The Archangel *[naqīb an-nuqabā']* appeared in his presence, although it had never appeared to him before then. As it beckoned to him, it said: "You must wish you had never been created, and that, having been created, you knew what you had been created for!"

O sleeper, you must wake up, for the waters of the flood are all around you. Who is your leader *[imām]*? On the Day of Resurrection you will be called to give evidence. What is your Scripture *[kitāb]*? Who is your teacher *[mu'allim]*? Who is your summoner *[dā'ī]*? Who is your Prophet *[nabī]*? You have no noble lineage *[nasab]*. Those whose lineage is authentic in the sight of Allāh and in the eyes of His Prophet (Allāh bless him and give him peace) are the people of dutiful devotion *[ahl at-taqwā]*. "O Messenger of Allāh," someone asked, "who are members of your family?" The Prophet (Allāh bless him and give him peace) replied:

> Every dutiful believer belongs to the family of Muḥammad *[kullu taqiyyin ālu Muḥammadin]*.

Hold your tongue, you have no common sense! Your house sits on the River Tigris and yet you are dying of thirst. Just two steps and you would reach the All-Merciful *[ar-Raḥmān]*. The lower self *[nafs]* and creatures [are the two things you need to step away from]. You too, O seeker! Just two steps and you would reach your goal in both this world and the hereafter.

If you wish for success *[falāḥ]*, you must endure with patience the hammer blows of my way of speaking. When my ecstasy *[junūn]* overtakes me, I cannot see you. When the temper *[ṭab']* of my innermost being *[sirr]* is aroused, the temper of my sincerity *[ikhlāṣ]*, I cannot see your face. I wish to improve you and to remove the dross from your heart. I shall put out the fire *[ḥarīq]* that threatens to burn your house down, and I shall protect the honor of your womenfolk *[ḥarīm]*.

Open your eyes and take notice of what is in front of you. The squads of punishment and chastisement have come to get you. Woe unto you, O stupid fool! You will very soon be dead. All that you are now involved in must fade away and be scattered. This fellow here will have to part *[yufāriqu]* with his children, his home and his wife, and then make friends *[yurāfiqu]* with the dust, the grave, and either the stokers of Hell *[zabāniya]* or the angels of mercy *[malā'ikat ar-raḥma]*. O passing traveler, O transient, O transferee, O temporary loan!

Glory be to the One who treats you all so kindly *[subḥāna man manna 'alaikum]*, O you who like to have fun without ever taking notice!

O you who forget your friends, not once a year do you bring me the tiniest trifle, let alone once a month or once a week. Take something for nothing, and tomorrow a million things. I am carrying your burdens, while you are scared that I might give you the job of bearing mine. Only Allāh (Almighty and Glorious is He) can take care of all my needs.

You say you would travel for a thousand years just to hear one word from me? But why, when the distance between me and you is only a few steps? You are lazy. You are a little ignoramus, a silly little fool. You think you have something to give. How many like you this world has fattened and then devoured! It made them plump with fame and fortune, then ate them up. If we had seen any good in it, you would not have beaten us to it.

> Do not all things come home to Allāh? (42:53)

As for what we are involved in, it all comes from Allāh (Exalted is He).

When the Shaikh had stepped down from the lectern, one of his pupils *[talāmidha]* said to him: "You were quite extreme in your admonition, and you spoke to him very harshly!" But the Shaikh replied: "If my words have had any effect upon him, he will surely come back for more." (The man did in fact attend the meeting *[majlis]* regularly from then on. He would also visit the Shaikh at other times, outside the formal session, and always behaved with the utmost humility and modesty in his presence. May Allāh the Exalted bestow His mercy upon him.)

O Allāh [grant us] patience and pardon! O Allāh, help us!

If you stand in the presence of any fellow creature, trying to obtain what he has at his disposal, Allāh will despise you.

[As the Prophet (Allāh bless him and give him peace) has said:]

> When someone pesters *[taḍa'ḍa'a]* a rich man, seeking what he has in his possession, two thirds of his religion are gone.

You have made a habit of trying to scrounge things from your fellow creatures, so you will be in that condition when you have to meet Allah (Exalted is He). One time in the public square I saw a man scrounging from the people, although he had just sold a *jubba*[14] of silk brocade for twenty-five dīnārs [gold coins]. So I followed him. He stopped beside a man who was eating *harīsa*[15], and would not leave him alone until he gave him a mouthful of it. I said to him: "Did you not sell a *jubba* for such and such a price?" His response was: "I am neglecting my trade because of you!"

When someone has progressed to the ultimate degree of saintship *[wilāya]*, he becomes a *Quṭb* [spiritual axis, pole or pivot]. As such, he must carry the burdens of all creatures put together, but he is given the equivalent of the faith *[īmān]* of all creatures put together, so that he will have the strength to bear what he must bear.

Pay no attention to my long shirt and my headcloth. This is what one wears after death. This is a shroud *[kafan]*, the shroud of the dead. This is what befits me now, after I have been accustomed to wearing coarse wool *[ṣūf]* and to eating rough or going hungry. I now have a pressing engagement, but not with any of you.

O people of Baghdād, be sensible! O people of the earth, O people of the heavens!

> And He creates what you do not know. (16:8)

It is not an affectation. This is an outward appearance *[ẓāhir]* that has an inner content *[bāṭin]* to prove its authenticity, and an inner reality that has an outer manifestation to confirm it.

[14] A *jubba* is a long outer garment, open at the front, with wide sleeves.

[15] *Harīsa* is a cooked dish of meat and crushed wheat, seasoned with spices and pepper.

There is nothing worth talking about until your lords *[arbāb]* become one single Lord *[Rabb]*, until your interests become single and the object of your love becomes single. Your heart must be unified. When will the nearness of the Lord of Truth pitch its tent in your heart? When will your heart come to be enraptured *[majdhūb]* and your innermost being *[sirr]* drawn near *[muqarrab]*, and when will you meet your Lord after taking your leave of creatures?

As Allāh's Messenger (Allāh bless him and give him peace) has said:

> If someone devotes himself entirely to Allāh (Almighty and Glorious is He), He will provide him with everything he needs, and if a person devotes himself entirely to this world, Allāh will leave him in its care.

[In the first of these cases], things will occur miraculously *[tukhraqu'l-'ādāt]* for his benefit. He will receive what Allāh has at His disposal, but only after total dedication to Him with his heart and his entire being *[kulliyya]*.

As Allāh (Exalted is He) has said:

> If anyone performs an action with the intention of involving someone other than Me [as a partner] in it, well, I am the more Independent of the two partners *[anā aghnā'sh-sharīkain]*. It [the action] involves the partner ascribed to Me *[sharīkī]* and has nothing to do with Me.[16]

Sincerity *[ikhlāṣ]* is the believer's plot of land, while his deeds *[a'māl]* are its surrounding walls. The walls are subject to alteration and change, but not so the ground. Only upon dutiful devotion *[taqwā]* can a building be firmly based.

If someone should say: "I have dedicated myself to Allāh (Almighty and Glorious is He), but He has not provided me with everything I need," the answer must be: "The fault lies in you, not in the Messenger."

[16] Variants of this Divine Saying *[ḥadīth qudsī]* have been recorded by several authorities, including Imām Muslim and Ibn Māja. See: William A. Graham, *Divine Word and Prophetic Word in Early Islam;* Mouton, The Hague and Paris, 1977; pp. 125–126.

Nor does he [the Messenger] speak from his own desire. (53:3)

Do you know anything at all about Allāh (Exalted is He)? No, by Allāh! You are all madly in love with this world and its glamour. If you were telling the truth about the claims you make, you would not have to resort to cunning tricks in order to obtain the merest trifle.

Cast your lower self *[nafs]* into the Valley of Destiny *[wādī'l-qadar]* until, when its time has come, the top rung of your ladder makes contact with the door of nearness [to the Lord]. You will be welcomed by a face more lovely than all the charming beauty of this world and the hereafter. The fond affection *[mawadda]* between the pair of you will be complete. All obstacles and intermediaries will disappear. Then you will hear its [the lower self's] call for help from the Valley of His Destiny: "Take charge of the deposits held in trust for you, and make full use of the service I can offer you. I am imprisoned over here, to your detriment or for your benefit." Your nearness [to the Lord] will plead on its behalf, urging a positive response to its request. At this point the hand of knowledge *['ilm]* will be extended to it, and the hand of the law *[ḥukm]* will come to its aid.

As for your immersion in it [this world] at the outset of your career, before you have mounted any opposition to your natural urges *[ṭab']*, your passions *[hawā]* and your willfulness *[irāda]*, in spite of your claim to be numbered among the loved ones *[maḥbūbūn]* and those who have been drawn near *[muqarrabūn]*, this is a regrettable delusion that will hold you back and an unfortunate error that will lead you astray. If you realized that this world was sure to leave you in the lurch, you would not ask so much of it. When your inner *[bāṭin]* becomes worthy to serve Allāh, only then will this world become fit to serve you. Its wine is poison; it may taste sweet at first, but it soon turns bitter. Once it has filtered through into your heart and you have come under its control, it converts into a poison and kills you.

Our predecessors would learn to distinguish between different kinds of notions *[khawāṭir]*, before withdrawing into secluded retreats *[zawāyā]*. O you who cannot tell the difference between the notion *[khāṭir]* of the lower self *[nafs]*, that of the devil *[shaiṭān]* and that of the heart *[qalb]*, how can you withdraw into seclusion? The satanic notion prompts one to commit sins of disobedience and to make mistakes; it implants the root of unbelief *[kufr]*, then encourages the sins of disobedience that branch out from it. As for the angelic notion *[khāṭir al-malak]*, it prompts one to practice worshipful obedience and to perform righteous deeds.

Somebody said to him who was crucified (meaning al-Ḥallāj): "Give me a piece of good advice!" He replied: "It concerns your lower self *[nafs]*; if you can control it, [well and good], otherwise it will control you."

If you wish to drink in the company of kings, you had better take to the empty ruins, the wastelands and the deserts, until you sober up from your intoxication, so that you do not divulge their secrets and have them put you to death for it. This is why it is better for them [the people of the Lord] to go wandering about, rather than settle down. This world has been put here as a means of transport, if you wish to meet your Lord.

Seclusion [is appropriate only] after [observance of] all the rules of the sacred law *[aḥkām ash-shar']*. The door of Allāh (Almighty and Glorious is He) cannot be reached without seeking help, and a firm determination to achieve something will make the means available. The door of knowledge *['ilm]* is arrived at by the path of the law *[ḥukm]*. The law means the [divine] commandments and prohibitions. We therefore accept what the law requires of us; we hear and we obey. At this stage we are exposed to adversities, so this is where the servant needs to be knowledgeable *['ālim]*. One of us may say: "Why should I have to suffer misfortune, despite my dedication to worshipful obedience?" Our response to him must be: "You need a little knowledge!"

The specialist in the law *[ṣāḥib al-ḥukm]* is concerned with storing the goods, while the specialist in knowledge *[ṣāḥib al-'ilm]* is concerned with their distribution. The law is associated with the pious abstainers *[zuhhād]*, while knowledge is associated with the champions of truth *[ṣiddīqūn]*, the loved ones, the intimate companions. Abstinence *[zuhd]* is associated with the law, while love is associated with knowledge. The one serves as a business partner *[sharīk]*, the other as a minister *[wazīr]*.

The ascetic *[mutazahhid]* is feverish *[maḥmūm]*, the pious abstainer *[zāhid]* is consumptive *[maslūl]* and he who has real knowledge *[ʿārif]* is alive after death. This ascetic has renounced the desires of the flesh and has been fasting, so his lower self *[nafs]* has caught a fever. The pious abstainer has experienced prolonged renunciation, so his sickness has been prolonged and has caused him to contract tuberculosis. This world has died as far as he is concerned. While he is lying in this condition on the bed of the gracious kindness of Allāh (Almighty and Glorious is He), what should appear at the door of his abstinence but food prepared in many different ways, as well as various styles of clothing hung on pegs! He cannot leave this world until he has received his allotted share in full. The unbelievers *[kuffār]* and disobedient sinners have not had the decency to seek [their proper due]; they have just helped themselves to things that are unlawful *[ḥarām]*.

Allāh (Exalted is He) gave that servant life, then He resurrected him as a different creature. Flesh had withered away, bone had weakened, skin had grown thin. The lower self *[nafs]* had lost its sweet taste, passion *[hawā]* had departed and natural inclination *[ṭabʿ]* had been overcome, while the heart contained the spirit *[rūḥ]*, the inner meaning *[maʿnā]*, the direct experience *[maʿrifa]* and the realization of Divine Unity *[tawḥīd]*.

Complete dominion belongs to the heart alone, and the Lord of Truth takes care of it. He brings His servant back to life after his death, his carnal desires and appetites having died a spiritual *[maʿnawī]* death. A symbolic death along with an actual death. Allāh brings him back to life after He has shown him what is over there. To the servant He has left dead at His door, He shows the vast scope of His wisdom and His mysteries, the multitude of His soldiers and His subjects. Then, when He has shown him His kingdom and informed him of His secret *[sirr]*, He joins his spirit *[rūḥ]* to his body and his outer *[ẓāhir]* to his inner *[bāṭin]*, so that he may receive his allotted shares *[aqsām]* in full. Prior to this, even if all the portions of the East and the West had been spread out before him, he could not have taken one single atom from them.

Through a mysterious power *[qudra khafīya]*, an inner will *[irāda bāṭina]* exerted by Allāh (Almighty and Glorious is He), His Prophets *[anbiyā']*, His saints *[awliyā']* and the special few *[khawāṣṣ]* among His creatures are detached from their worldly desires. Not the slightest trace of carnal desire and willfulness remains within them, so that their inner beings *[bawāṭin]* are purely devoted to Him. Then, when He wishes to grant them their allotted shares in full, He creates the life of worldly existence *[wujūd]* within them, so that all the allotted shares may be received.

Jesus (peace be upon him) did not marry; he never took a wife. At the end of time, Allāh (Exalted is He) will send him back down to the earth, and He will then marry him to a young woman of Quraish,[17] who will bear him a son.

As for the person with real experience *['ārif]*, he does not receive his portion until after achieving proficiency in both knowledge *['ilm]* and abstinence *[zuhd]*, then he collects his allotted shares along with all the rest of you. He regains his worldly appetites after having abstained from them [to be on the safe side] whenever there was any doubt. Once he has acquired knowledge, cold water tastes good to him, while in the eyes of pious abstainers the finest meal seems like drinking wine and eating the flesh of the pig. Many a pious abstainer is shut off by his abstinence from the Lord of Truth, and many a person with real experience is shut off through dwelling too much on his experience *[ma'rifa]*, although this is actually rather unusual and in most cases he is likely to be safe and sound.

As a general rule, your closeness to the sons of this world keeps you far away from Allāh (Almighty and Glorious is He). The right course for you is to concentrate your attention on the hereafter and on worshipful obedience, then you may be saved, while your allotted shares will come to you even if they are unwelcome.

[17] Quraish is the name of the Arab tribe into which the Prophet Muḥammad (Allāh bless him and give him peace) was born.

What He requires of you [first of all] is that you stop following your natural tendency *[ṭab']* and put in its place the special concessions *[rukhaṣ]* allowed by the sacred law *[shar']*. Then He will instruct you to give up these special concessions bit by bit, until all your actions are in accordance with the strict interpretation *['azīma]*. Then, if you patiently observe the strict version of the law, love for Allāh (Almighty and Glorious is He) will arise within your heart. Once love is firmly established there, saintship *[wilāya]* will come to you from Allāh (Almighty and Glorious is He).

If you are sensible, count yourself among the people of the Fire [of Hell], because this will encourage you to improve your conduct. If you are in fact one of the people of the Garden [of Paradise], you will have demonstrated your gratitude to Him. When you go out of your house, you should feel as if you were going forth to war, as if you might never come back home again. You should also be aware that you are made to suffer because of your acquisitiveness, and be convinced that Allāh (Exalted is He) is capable of sustaining you without effort or strain.

The believer *[mu'min]* is sometimes like a mountain and at other times like a feather, blown about by the winds of His destiny *[qadar]*; in the face of misfortunes like a mountain, but in the company of the Lord of Truth (Almighty and Glorious is He) like a feather wafted by the winds of His decrees *[aqdār]*.

O people of ours, it is too late for you to fill the role of Messenger *[risāla]* or the role of Prophet *[nubuwwa]*, but there is still time for you to experience saintship *[wilāya]*!

There can be no access to the King's company as long as one is still attached to worldly existence *[wujūd]*. It seems you must be blind, since you do not see. It seems you must have quenched your thirst, since you do not drink. It seems you must be dead, since there is no movement in you. Woe unto the outcasts who are unaware of being outcasts! You do no good, nor do you help the good people to do good. You are bad; you love a worldly life with no hereafter, an outer *[ẓāhir]* with no inner *[bāṭin]*. You will gain no benefit from your important connections, your wealth and your patron. You will soon be dead, and after death you will suffer humiliation.

> Should anyone desire glory, the glory belongs to Allāh. (35:10)

And [thus it also belongs] to His Messenger *[rasūl]* and to the saints *[awliyā']* and the champions of truth *[ṣiddīqūn]*.

The ocean is this world, the ship is the sacred law *[shar']* and the sailor is the grace *[lutf]* of Allāh (Almighty and Glorious is He). Anyone who deviates from following the sacred law will therefore drown in this world, but if someone seeks refuge aboard the ship of the sacred law and makes himself at home there, the sailor will appoint him to be his lieutenant *[istanābahu]*. He will put him in charge of the ship and everything aboard it, and will make him a relative by finding him a bride from his own family *[ṣāharahu]*. This is how it will be for someone who forsakes this world, devotes himself to the acquisition of knowledge *['ilm]*, bears suffering with patience and comes to be the beloved *[maḥbūb]* of the sacred law. While he is in this condition, lo and behold, Allāh (Almighty and Glorious is He) will come and bestow His grace upon him. He will grant him His intimate knowledge *[ma'rifa]* and invest him with robes of honor specially designed for him. One mark of divine friendship on top of another *[wilāya fawqa wilāya]*!

In Allāh you have ample compensation for the loss of anything other than Him. If something happens to pass you by, do not feel sad about it, for the King disposes of His property as He sees fit. The slave *['abd]* belongs to his Master *[Mawlā]*, along with everything he owns. Whatever He may take away from you, you will find it again tomorrow [at the Resurrection]. The Fire [of Hell] will say: "Pass through, O believer *[mu'min]*, for your light has extinguished my flames!" Likewise in this world, when faith *[īmān]* has grown strong and one's inner being *[bāṭin]* has made contact with the nearness of the Lord of Truth (Almighty and Glorious is He), along comes the fire of disasters to cause an obstruction on the path of hearts. The fire of conflicts takes its stand on the path of aspirants, then it catches the aspirant *[murīd]* because of the remnants he still carries, traces of worldly attachment and attention to creatures. To those of perfect faith *[kāmil al-īmān]* it says: "Pass through, O believer, for your light has extinguished my flames!" They are not injured in this world by arrows that fall from the castle walls. You must conduct yourselves in such a way that neither the fire of this world nor that of the hereafter will be able to harm you.

Allāh (Almighty and Glorious is He) has certain servants whom He calls physicians *[aṭibbā']*. He lets them live in good health *['āfiya]*, causes them to die in good health and admits them to the Garden [of Paradise] in good health.

When someone really knows *['arafa]* Allāh (Almighty and Glorious is He), he becomes detached from carnal appetites and pleasures. It is only because he is compelled to do so that he accepts all his allotted shares [of worldly goods]. "The neighbor before the house *[al-jār qabla'd-dār]*." Having won the neighbor, this fortunate person *[mubārak]* now gains the house, established in possession by the King. The King has said:

> You are today in our presence established and worthy of trust. (12:54)

When someone has really come to know Allāh, and has been admitted to His presence, he will not reach out with his eyes or his hands toward anything in His kingdom. He is just like a bride *['arūs]* who has been solemnly escorted to the King. Her food and drink are the nearness of the King. In His nearness she finds the fulfillment of all her desires. When the lower self *[nafs]* has become obedient, it melts together with the heart, which becomes its jailer. Then the King releases the heart from the prison.

> And the king said: "Bring him to me." (12:50)

After his nobility and his good character and good conduct have become apparent, he is will be escorted into His presence. He will greet him with noble generosity, draw him near and bring him close, treat him kindly, invest him with robes of honor and address him without an intermediary, saying:

> You are today in our presence established and worthy of trust.

He will keep all his attention focused on Himself.

At this point the Shaikh (may Allāh be well pleased with him) gave a loud cry, then he said:

O Allāh, O Allāh, O Allāh! An absent friend has arrived.

He will entertain him so that he cannot be distracted. When he has been in His company for quite some time, and the weariness of his journey has left him, he will put on flesh again and his bones will recover their strength. Life will be pleasant for him and his unsettled feelings will calm down. He will come to be the confidential servant *[biṭāna]* of the King. At this stage He will appoint him to a position of authority, putting him in command of His subjects, His followers and His territory. He will send him on missions *[arsalahu]* at sea, to rescue the drowning, and on dry land, to snatch both grown men and children from the jaws of wild beasts.

Once he had left the house of his natural inclination *[ṭab']*, He considered him fit for delegated authority *[niyāba]* and trusteeship *[amāna]*. On the hearts of such servants He confers robes of honor, just as he conferred them on the hearts of the Prophets *[nabiyyūn]* and Messengers *[mursalūn]*, and their titles *[alqāb]* are the titles of the saints *[awliyā']* and the *abdāl*.

O rabble! Here we have the confidential servants *[baṭā'in]* of kings, the friends of the élite *[aṣḥāb al-akhyār]*! (By this he was alluding to the saints *[awliyā']* and angels *[malā'ika]* who had come to attend his meeting *[majlis]*, although they were invisible to the rest of the audience, who were unaware of their presence.)

Question: When does expansion *[basṭ]* give way to constriction *[qabḍ]*, and having fun to being serious?

As long as He is going easy on you *[bāsaṭaka]*, you can take it easy *[inbasaṭta]*. Then your license to enjoy concessions *[rukhṣa]* will be converted into strict attention to duty *['azīma]*, and then your strict performance will become a pleasure, until eventually, when the whole of you has become strictly devoted to duty, He will cause you to enter the abode of gracious favor *[faḍl]* and intimate friendship *[uns]*. All that is left for you then will be action pure and simple *[fi'l mujarrad]*, with no question of either concession or strictness. Your situation will be comparable to that of a person who has in front of him a dish containing a bit of food, and who is then told: "Go into a different house. Everything over there is for you." Concessions are for those who have made little progress, while strict requirements are for those who are fully developed *[kāmil]*, and the Kingdom is for those who have transcended this worldly existence *[fānūn]*.

Previously, I always dwelt here on earth in private seclusion, but now the situation is the very opposite of that. In general, I am a person who is not embarrassed by being talked about, because I take no notice of anyone's opinion.

Proper behavior *[ḥusn al-adab]* is called for in two instances: in the renunciation of this world and in the acceptance of it. You must not go into seclusion with ignorance for company. Do not make a practice of it before you are adequately prepared. "Complete your studies, then retire *[tafaqqah thumma' 'tazil]*." How often do you attend these sessions *[majālis]* without putting one word you hear into practice? How many of you have seen a single saint *[walī]*, asked him for a piece of good advice, received such advice from him and then put it into practice, taking it as provision for your journey?

As for you there, you pore over the annals *[akhbār]*, you peer into the traditions *[āthār]*, you attend the sessions of divine remembrance *[majālis al-adhkār]*, yet you make no progress at all. If only you could hold your footing at the point you have already reached, but no, whenever you come forward you go into reverse.

If there is no difference for a person between one day and the next, he must be a dimwit. Come to your senses! May Allāh have mercy upon you! This world can offer only momentary satisfaction, so do not rely on it.

There are some people who have been rendered weak by awe and dread, whose limbs have been rendered immobile and whose hearts have been overwhelmed by bewilderment at the creation, so that they have come to be a state of paralysis and inactivity. When the time comes for them to receive their full quota of allotted shares, Allāh sends someone to feed them bit by bit.

No one past or present has anything to hold against this servant (meaning himself). Preserve the most important part of your religion *[dīn]*, or else you must sever your connection with me and my path. Do not be an ignorant fool, sitting at home and indulging in your fantasies. Here we have medicines that we have drunk and found beneficial. Here we have something tried and tested, to which we can show you the way.

Beware of a day when neither wealth nor sons will be of any avail! What is wealth? Wealth is something you have accumulated from what has fallen due to you and what you have managed to acquire, and you have acquired it by any means. You claim that tomorrow [at the Resurrection] it will stand you in good stead, along with all the sons you have, just as the Arabs in the old days used to claim.

But Allāh (Almighty and Glorious is He) has said:

> The day when neither wealth nor sons will avail [any man], except one who comes to Allāh with a whole heart. (26:88, 89)

Such a person will not have paid too much attention with his heart to his worldly goods and his sons. Rather than letting his heart rely on them, he will have recognized that he was entrusted with their care. He will have looked after them in order to comply with the wishes of his Lord. Thus his heart would be safe from the perils that come with having wealth and children.

Consider the case of a man who is informed that the king wishes to marry him to a slave girl, and that he intends to have him killed by her hand. The man says to himself: "If I try to run away, the king will catch me with his soldiers. If I refuse to obey him, he has the power to destroy me, but if I comply with his wishes, he will destroy me anyway, by means of his slave girl." The king does in fact command him to marry one of his slave girls, and he orders her to poison him or to slit his throat when he has fallen asleep.—Oh, how much is being missed by those who have stayed away from me today! Oh, how much they are missing!—But the best thing he can do is to behave politely and show himself ready to comply with the royal command, while keeping his heart on the alert. "To hear is to obey," says he, and in he goes to accept the marriage and the gift *[hadiyya]*. The wedding night *[zifāf]* has arrived. He dons the armor of caution. He anoints the eyes of his heart with the ointment of wakefulness, to make sure that he will notice her every movement, pause and action. She turns out to be his joy and delight, and the attendants and servants all think he must have found himself in an enviable situation. When the new day dawns, she has not murdered him with her poison!

> ...except one who comes to Allāh with a whole heart *[bi-qalbin salīm]*. (26:89)

This world is the wife in whose company he has not fallen asleep, and with whom he has never in his life been alone in private. He has reached the hereafter, and she has neither robbed him of his dutiful devotion *[taqwā]* nor altered his religion. That is keeping safe and whole *[salāma]*! It is like this for one who really knows *[ʿārif]* Allāh, who abstains from this world and yearns for the hereafter. The messenger of knowledge *[rasūl al-ʿilm]* comes into the pure serenity of his innermost being *[sirr]* with this information: "Allāh wishes to assign to you a group of people from this world, so that there may be life for the hearts of the champions of truth *[ṣiddīqūn]*. This is a kind of task, one that requires labor and trouble and attention. Be careful how you perform it. Your heart and your innermost being *[sirr]* must be sound and whole, so the innermost being must be fully conscious of this." The innermost being and the heart are escorted together to the King's door. They ask: "What do You propose to do with us? Do You intend to exclude us from Your presence, to banish us from your door, to make life painful for us?

We shall not leave without the proper assurances *[mawāthīq]* and covenants *['uhūd].*" They will not leave until He says to them:

> Fear not, for I am with you both. I hear and I see. (20:46)

Then they will return together to this world, accompanied by escorts and guards.

> ...except one who comes to Allāh with a whole heart. (26:89)

[Such a heart is sound and free] from harmful influences, from pretense and hypocrisy and the desire to impress mere creatures.

O seeker far from home, O wanderer lost in the trackless wilderness of destiny *[qadar]*! You need to tidy up your private room. Leave in it neither dirham [silver coin] nor dīnār [gold coin], and as for jewelry you have enough with the key in your pocket. You need to empty your heart of this world, of carnal appetites and pleasures and trivial concerns of every kind. You must let it contain only remembrance *[dhikr]* and contemplation *[fikr]*, the remembrance of death and the remembrance of what lies beyond death. In it you must practice the alchemy *[kīmiyā']* of curtailing expectation. You must say: "I am already dead," because actions become pure through the curtailment of expectation *[qaṣr al-amal].*

If you exaggerate your expectation, on the other hand, you will be seeking to make an impression on this person here, and behaving hypocritically toward that person there. Someone who has mastered the curtailment of expectation is separated from everything, disconnected from everything. He wears the garb of abstinence *[zuhd]*, then the garb of annihilation *[fanā']*, then the garb of real experience *[ma'rifa].*

Allāh's Messenger (Allāh bless him and give him peace) has said:

> Guarantee me six things and I will guarantee you the Garden [of Paradise]: When one of you talks, he must not tell lies; when he is trusted, he must not cheat; when he makes a promise, he must not break it; you must restrain your hands [from evil deeds]; you must not look for trouble; and you must keep your genitals safe.

When your innermost being *[sirr]* has become pure and unified, you will hear the call of your Lord directly, without any intermediary. When your fear and your hope have been united, the speech of your Lord *[Rabb]* and Master *[Mawlā]* will address you.

O my dear son, cast yourself down in front of the hoofs of the horse of His destiny *[qadar]*; it will either trample you or leap over you. "If someone suffers destruction *[talaf]* because of Allāh, his compensation *[khalaf]* is Allāh's responsibility." If it does leap over you, catch hold of it and cling on, exposing yourself to the arrows of His destiny. When you become a target for the arrows of His destiny, their impact will only cause a scratch, not a fatal wound.

O you who are destitute of all this, you must improve, make progress and set to work. Get to grips with it all. Give up your bad habit of sitting at home while I am sitting down to give a talk. Here are the qualities of saintship *[wilāyāt]*. Here are the degrees *[darajāt]*.

O you who are afflicted with the burden of having dependants to provide for, let your earning be devoted to your dependants and your heart to the gracious favor of your Lord. For one group of people, their lawful goods *[ḥalāl]* are acquired though what they earn. There are people whose lawful goods are what they obtain in answer to their supplication *[du'ā']*. There are people whose lawful goods are what they receive from others without having to ask, and then there are people whose lawful goods are what they get by begging. This is the state of affairs during training *[riyāḍa]*, which cannot go on indefinitely.

The first case, namely earning, is in accordance with the Sunna. The second, namely asking [in prayers of supplication], is of weak validity. The third, [accepting what comes without asking], is the approach that is strictly correct *['azīma]*.

As for begging, this is allowed as a special concession *[rukhṣa]*. It may happen that someone goes begging when he is not in need, in which case he represents a trial and a tribulation for the person asked to give. The request made by this servant [of the Lord] is like the request that comes in the night.

The Prophet (Allāh bless him and give him peace) has said:

> Do not reject the request that comes in the night, for someone who is neither a jinnī nor a human being may come to you, in order to see how you are handling the blessings that Allāh (Almighty and Glorious is He) has bestowed upon you.

In just the same way, this servant is commanded to ask, so that the Lord of Truth may see how you are handling the blessings that He has bestowed upon you.

Make a frequent practice of attending the sessions *[majālis]* of the scholars and of visiting the tombs and the righteous *[ṣāliḥūn]*, then perhaps your heart will be brought to life.

Once they [the people of the Lord] have become thoroughly proficient in carrying out the commandments and observing the prohibitions [of the sacred law], the decrees of destiny *[aqdār]* come to their aid. 'Abdullāh ibn az-Zubair used to eat one meal a week. Your spiritual state *[ḥāl]* will not be correct until you are like a cracked pot in which no liquid can remain. Consider the example of the ship belonging to some poor folk, which was boarded by *al-Khiḍr*, who damaged it and then passed on to another situation. There is one state of being that features integration *[jam']* and there is another that features differentiation *[tafriqa]*, as there is one state that features paucity *[qilla]* and another that features multiplicity *[kathra]*.

If someone goes out of my presence in the direction of the Fire [of Hell], may Allāh have no mercy on him!

O Allāh, pardon! O Allāh, protection! O Allāh, steadfastness! O Allāh, contentment!

When you attain to the Lord of Truth (Almighty and Glorious is He), He will be satisfied with you as long as you perform the *farā'iḍ* [obligatory religious duties, as distinguished from those that are merely commendable or supererogatory].

The King's cook is now an old man. No longer can he think, see, hear and give instructions [as he did in his prime]. He must now have done for him what he could do himself in his active condition.

Let Allāh be your witness, O seeker, if you are speaking the truth about the claims you make. When have you ever used your strength for your neighbor's benefit rather than your own? When have you offered him your shirt, your turban and your prayer-mat *[muṣallā]* before using them yourself? When have you put your wealth at his disposal first of all?

These people [of the Lord] have dissolved their lower selves *[nufūs]*, their natural impulses *[ṭibā']*, their passions *[ahwiya]* and their tastes *[sharāb]*, to the point where they have died in the spiritual sense *[ma'nan]*, where they have become extinct *[fanū]* in the spiritual sense. The hand of [divine] power *[qudra]* has taken control of them. The mortician *[ghāsil]* of destiny *[qadar]* rolls them over to right and to left,

> while their dog is stretching out its paws on the threshold. (18:18)

The remnants of the lower self are stretched out beneath the threshold of destiny.

The medication prescribed for the limbs and organs of the physical body is to refrain from sins *[ma'āthim]*; that is to say, from perpetrating atrocious misdeeds and offenses. Your hand must refrain from stealing and striking, while the foot must refrain from walking into sinful disobedience, and from walking toward the worldly ruler *[sulṭān]* or indeed any of the children of Adam. This eye of yours must be restrained from looking at pretty women.

The lower self *[nafs]* has become calm and quiet in the presence of the law *[ḥukm]*. The heart has flown off into the company of the Beloved *[maḥbūb]*.

If the friend *[walī]* of Allāh (Exalted is He) behaves correctly, he will acquire the attributes *[ṣifāt]* of Prophethood *[nubuwwa]*.

The law *[ḥukm]* fluctuates between nature *[ṭab']* and knowledge *['ilm]*, sometimes rejecting nature and sometimes rejecting knowledge.

> Whatever the Messenger gives you, take it. (59:7)

The law says to the heart: "What will supply your needs? I am standing at the ready, like a servant at your disposal, a guardian to look after you, while you are in the company of the King."

The night is their royal throne. The private retreat is their bridal chamber. The day excites their interest in certain material means *[asbāb]*.

Afflictions ought to be kept secret:

> O my dear son, do not narrate your vision to your brothers. (12:5)

You must be strong in dealing with them. Protect one another and support one another until the book [of destiny] reaches its appointed conclusion.

Ask *Munkar* and *Nakīr*[18] about me when they come to visit you in your grave, for they will tell you all you need to know about me. Your present name is *Mudhnib* [sinner]. Tomorrow [at the Resurrection] your name will be *Muḥāsab* [called to account] and *Munāqash* [subject to interrogation]. In the grave you must suffer having all your faults exposed. You do not know whether you will be included among the people of the Fire [of Hell] or among the people of the Garden [of Paradise]. Your ultimate destination is uncertain, so do not overestimate the purity of your spiritual state *[ḥāl]*. You do not know what your name is going to be tomorrow.

O my dear son, if you are still alive in the morning, do not take the evening for granted, and if you are here when evening comes, do not take the next morning for granted. Yesterday is past and gone with everything it contained, to be a witness for you and against you [when the Resurrection comes]. As for tomorrow, you do not know whether you will survive till then or not. You are simply the son of your today. How stupidly careless you are! The symptom of your heedlessness is your addiction to foolish company.

[18] *Munkar* and *Nakīr* are the two angels charged with the interrogation of the dead. Their names do not occur in the Qur'ān, but they are mentioned in a saying of the Prophet (Allāh bless him and give him peace), in which their work is described in some detail.

O stupid fool, why do you associate with those on whom the mark of the Truth *[Ḥaqq]* is not apparent? Why do you seek the company of someone whose foundation is unstable, whose outer *[ẓāhir]* is all lower self *[nafs]*, and whose inner *[bāṭin]* is all stubbornness and insolence toward the Lord of Truth (Almighty and Glorious is He)? This [business of ours] is not something that comes about through rubbing shoulders, nor through anointing the eyes with cosmetics *[kuḥl]* but not with sleepless vigil.

The entire creation is of no consequence. All nonessential effort *[takalluf]* is of no consequence. O stupid fool, you go around begging from door to door, in order to accumulate a mass of worldly stuff. How can you have any hope of real success *[falāḥ]*? Why not stand at the King's door like the chamberlain *[ḥājib]*, informing the King of new arrivals, listening to their stories and making them feel less lonely? Why not treat your fellow creatures as your dependants, instead of depending on them? Why not work at your craft or profession in your own home, so that when they come to your door they will discover that you have something useful to offer them? Your home is your private retreat, your home is your heart, your home is your secret soul *[sirr]*, your home is your inner being *[bāṭin]*.

To deserve the company of your Lord, you must carry out His commandments, observe His prohibitions and comply with His wishes by accepting whatever has been decreed *[maqdūr]* by Him.

The blessings bestowed on your fellow creatures are in proportion to your prayer of supplication *[du'ā']* and your spiritual aspiration *[himma]*, in the ratio of a thousand to one. When you honor the virtuous noble ones in your private retreat, you are obeying your Master *[Mawlā]* and not offending against Him. If you honor the people [of the Lord] and do not disgrace yourself in their sight, you deserve to be called noble *[karīm]*. Then, once you have come to be noble, a thousand individuals will be honored for your sake. Misfortune will be averted from your family, your neighbor and the people of your town.

You are always begging. You are always going to people's doors. How long will it be before others can beg from you? How long before others can expect a meal from you? How long before they can come to your door? When will you be finished with your business? When will a tent be pitched around you? When will you celebrate your wedding in the close presence of the King? When will you demonstrate your excellence, your worthiness and your fitness for the proximity of the King? When will your titles *[alqāb]* be made known and your magnificence be revealed? When will you be the noblest of the noblest of the descendants of Muḥammad (Allāh bless him and give him peace), so that his blessed grace *[baraka]* may be conferred upon you?

[As the Prophet (Allāh bless him and give him peace) has said:]

> The learned scholars *['ulamā']* are the heirs of the Prophets *[anbiyā']*.

[They are their heirs] in speech and in action, in spiritual state *[ḥāl]* and in teaching *[maqāl]*, not in name and title. Prophethood *[nubuwwa]* is a name *[ism]*, while Messengership *[risāla]* is a title *[laqab]*. O ignorant one, although Prophethood and Messengership have passed you by, it is not yet too late for you to experience Saintship *[wilāya]* and attain to the stations of Ghawth *[ghawthiyya]* and Badal *[badaliyya]* .

[In the words of Allāh (Almighty and Glorious is He):]

> Are you content with the life of this world, rather than the hereafter? (9:38)

The life of this world *[ḥayāt ad-dunyā]* is your lower self *[nafs]*, your passions *[hawā]* and your natural inclinations *[ṭab']*. This is what is meant by this world—not carnal appetites *[shahawāt]* of brief duration, for they are portions allotted to you by destiny *[aqsām]*. This world is what you take hold of with your own mental and physical powers *[bi-himmatika wa-jawāriḥika]*. What the King imposes upon you does not count as belonging to this world. Vital necessities do not count as belonging to this world, for you cannot do without a house to provide you with shelter, clothes to cover and protect you, bread to satisfy your hunger and a wife to make you feel at home. Living the life of this world means devoting one's attention to creatures and turning one's back on the Lord of Truth.

Passion *[hawā]* is at odds with rational contemplation *[fikr]*. Passion is at odds with worshipful service *['ibāda]*. The material means *[sabab]* is at odds with the Originator *[Musabbib]*. The outer *[ẓāhir]* is at odds with the inner *[bāṭin]*. Once you have mastered the outer, you will be commanded to master the inner. Once you have mastered the law *[ḥukm]* by putting it into practice, you will be His servant, you will be His follower, you will be His companion *[ṣāḥib]*. You will be constitutionally extinct to your natural inclinations. Knowledge *['ilm]* will hold your reins, to keep you tightly in control. You will be like a husband between two spouses. You will be like the chamberlain *[ḥājib]* between the king and his chief minister *[wazīr]*. You will be the beloved of this world and of the hereafter, of creatures and of the Lord of Truth (Almighty and Glorious is He) and the angels *[malā'ika]*, a joy to all hearts. We experience a state of being that is beyond your present awareness.

David said to his son Solomon (peace be upon them both, and upon all the Prophets *[anbiyā']*, the Messengers *[mursalūn]*, the angels drawn near [to the Lord], the saints *[awliyā']* and the righteous *[ṣāliḥūn]*): "O my dear son, how vile is sinful error after humble submission *[maskana]*, and how much worse than that is a man who used to be a worshipper *['ābid]*, but who then abandoned the worshipful service *['ibāda]* of his Lord."

> Are you content with the life of this world, rather than the hereafter? (9:38)

The life of this world is your personal existence *[wujūd]*, while the hereafter is your nonexistence *[fanā']*.

Our aspirations *[himam]* have a way of undergoing change, and our innermost beings *[asrār]* also have their way of experiencing transformation. The common people *['awāmm]* have a way of going through changes, and the special few *[khawāṣṣ]* also have their way of experiencing transformation.

This world is what you can see, while the hereafter is that which is revealed *[yuftaḥu]* to you. You are presented with something you cannot comprehend, so you feel bewildered, but then all is made clear to you. When something presents itself to you as a matter of common sense *['aql mushtarak]*, it is of this world, but if something comes to you in terms peculiar to the intellect which is the intellect of intellects *['aql al-'uqūl]*, then it is of the hereafter. Your innermost being *[sirr]* is otherworldly, while your outer *[ẓāhir]* is this-worldly. The involvements of this world are with everything apart from the Lord of Truth (Almighty and Glorious is He), whereas the hereafter is attachment to the Master *[Mawlā]*, and indifference to tittle-tattle *[qīl wa-qāl]*, to praise and approval as well as to blame, and to the pursuit of self-interest. "Your interest is what is important to you *[hammuka mā hammaka]*."

If you are sincere about your purpose, the Lord of Truth (Almighty and Glorious is He) will take you by your hand. He will cause you to walk in the company of His destiny *[qadar]*, and the strides you make will be longer than the strides of Adam (blessing and peace be upon him), because of the sincerity *[ṣidq]* of your purpose *[irāda]*, the excellence of your behavior, and the way you turn a deaf ear to whatever your neighbors may have to say.

Let perdition befall you, O ignorant one, ignorant of the Lord of Truth, of the fact that His gracious favor is all around you, of the presence of His servants who have heard and obeyed!

The servant [of the Lord] sees his own allotted shares on the Preserved Tablet *[al-lawḥ al-maḥfūẓ]*, then he moves on to see the shares allotted to his wife and his children. Eventually, when he is lost in amazement, he hears a voice calling from his inner being *[bāṭin]*:

> He is only a servant on whom We bestowed favor. (43:59)

> And surely in Our sight they are among the chosen, the excellent. (38:47)

This is something that comes about through preordainment *[sābiqa]*; it can then be purified by following in the footsteps of the Shaikhs.

The Shaikh (may Allāh be well pleased with him) was deep in his state of rapture *[samāʿ]* and ecstasy *[wajd]*, when he was handed a slip of paper with a question concerning a point of Islamic jurisprudence *[masʾala fiqhiyya]* written on it. He said: "[I must ask you to wait] until I get permission to speak on the subject, and while I see what occurs to me." Then he said:

Is marriage a necessary duty *[wājib]*, or not? On this question there is a lack of consensus [among the leading Islamic jurists]. There are those who maintain that dedication to worship is preferable, in the case of a person whose lower self *[nafs]* does not experience a strong desire [for sexual intercourse]. Such is the view held by ash-Shāfiʿī and Aḥmad [ibn Ḥanbal], while according to Abū Ḥanīfa there is greater merit in devoting oneself to marriage.

Where you are concerned, as long as you are a seeker *[murīd]*, it is more appropriate for you to concentrate on your worshipful service *[ʿibāda]*. If you are one who is sought *[murād]*, on the other hand, it is not for you to manage your personal affairs; if He so wills, He will find you a wife, and if He so wills, He will keep you occupied in other directions.

If there is an allotment [in your destiny], you will obtain it in due course. The allotted portion *[qism]* will try to grab you by the tail, then it will say to the Lord of Truth: "Relieve me of my responsibility toward this fellow! He keeps running away from me, despite the fact that You have allotted me to him. What am I to do, since he will not pay any attention to me?" Then He will make you take notice of it.

As for the seeker *[murīd]*, marriage is unlawful *[ḥarām]* for him from the point of view of the inner *[bāṭin]*. Does he have a spare shirt to offer, or four inches of land? This is a traveler, whose only property is perseverance *[thabāt]*, not clothes *[thiyāb]* and not furniture *[athāth]*. He is actually stripped bare of all his own clothes. Once he has reached his destination, however, and his traveling days are over, if his King wishes him to take a wife, He will make him the owner of property; He can provide for him, as He can keep him deprived.

Anyone who makes friends with a fool must be a fool himself. The fool is someone who does not really know *[lam yaʿrif]* Allāh (Almighty and Glorious is He). He is content with the life of this world, rather than the hereafter.

O young man! Your allotted portion *[qism]* will not be used up by anyone else. Do not take your food from the hand of Satan and devour it to satisfy your natural urges *[ṭabʿ]* and your passions *[hawā]*. It is better for you to wait awhile, until you attain to your abode in the Garden [of Paradise], or to the nearness of your Lord.

A man said to him: "From the time when I was very young, right up until recently, I always performed a special act of private prayer and recitation *[wird]*.[19] But now, I stand up, I perform two cycles of prayer *[arkaʿu rakʿatain]*, then I collapse in a faint before I have time to complete my devotions."

The Shaikh (may Allāh be well pleased with him) responded by saying:

There is no cause for alarm. It is not a stroke of the evil eye *[naẓra]*, but a stroke of preordainment *[sābiqa]*. The eye of a champion of truth *[ṣiddīq]* caught sight of you in the course of his passage to the Lord of Truth (Almighty and Glorious is He). Since he approved of what he saw in you, he said to his brethren *[ikhwān]*: "Take him along in your company!"

[As the Prophet (Allāh bless him and give him peace) has said:]

> In the days of your lifetime Allāh surely has gifts *[nafaḥāt]* to offer. You should indeed be ready to receive His gifts.

[19] Etymologically, the term *wird* [plural: *awrād*] means "to go down to a watering-place." In the context of Islāmic worship, it refers to a definite time of day or night devoted to private prayer (over and above the five daily prayers at their prescribed times), as well as to the 'litany' recited on this occasion. In its simplest form, the *wird* consists of four cycles *[rakaʿāt]* of prayer, with the recitation of one seventh of the Qurʾān.

There is no cause for alarm. Your heart has grown old, and its King has made it sit down at the door of His nearness. There is no cause for alarm. The outer *[ẓāhir]* has grown weak, but the inner *[bāṭin]* has grown strong. There is no cause for alarm. The bones of your heart have grown feeble and its skin has worn thin, but the vigilant care and gracious kindness [of the Lord] have seized hold of its innermost being *[sirr]*. Your heart can see the door of your Lord. The awe inspired by His nearness has overwhelmed it and made it swoon.

In preserving the integrity of the heart there is indeed a job to keep one fully occupied. One tiny fraction of the deeds of the heart is a thousand times better than all the deeds of the outer *[ẓāhir]*. As long as you have not neglected the obligatory religious duties *[farā'iḍ]* and the Sunna, you need fear no harm.

Someone once said to al-Junaid: "The urban dweller *[ḥaḍarī]* is operating a mill, around which he revolves without eating or drinking." He replied: "Observe his condition at the times of the [five] prescribed prayers *[ṣalawāt]*," and the response to this was: "When the muezzin *[mu'adhdhin]* gives the call to prayer, he takes a break." "So there is nothing to worry about," said al-Junaid.

Among them [the people of the Lord] there are those who are capable of performing tasks *[a'māl]* from the time when they are very young right up to the moment of death. There are others who keep working until they become too weak. If this is due to nearness [to the Lord], to knowledge *['ilm]*, to visionary experience *[mushāhada]*, then there is nothing wrong. If it is due to some other cause, however, it must be a devil *[shaiṭān]* that is leading him astray and a lower self *[nafs]* that is molesting him.

The companionship of the law *[ḥukm]* gives rise to knowledge *['ilm]*. It gives them access to the secret realm *[sirr]*. Have you any clue about this? You must become detached, then become connected. Become connected *[ittaṣil]*, then connect *[awṣil]*.

How great is the loss of those who waste their time in the shops of greedy ambition, expectation and reputation! Your innermost being *[sirr]* will surely die, and your heart will turn dark.

As the Prophet (Allāh bless him and give him peace) has said:

> Hearts do indeed get rusty, and the polish to make them shine is the recitation of the Qur'ān.

O Allāh, guide us aright and let others receive right guidance through us! Have mercy on us and let others receive mercy through us! Grant us real knowledge *['arrifnā]* and let others gain real knowledge through us! Let me be blessed with grace *[mubārak]* wherever I may be!

Become connected *[ittaṣil]*, then become disconnected *[infaṣil]*, then make connections *[awṣil]*. "Complete your studies, then retire *[tafaqqah thumma 'tazil]*." If someone tries to worship Allāh in a state of ignorance, he will do more harm than good. You must take along with you the lantern of your Lord's sacred law *[shar']*. By the light of the law *[ḥukm]*, you will enter into the domain of knowledge *['ilm]*.

Stop depending on material means *[asbāb]*. Part company with brethren and neighbors. As for the shares allotted by destiny *[aqsām]*, it serves no purpose to abstain from them. Present your back to your wife. Present the allotted shares with your back. Act like an ascetic *[tazahhad]*, then practice abstinence *[zuhd]* in earnest. Practice renunciation *[i'rāḍ]* in earnest. Give up your greedy appetite. Refine your behavior. You must be detached from everything apart from Him, dissociated from other creatures and from material means, always afraid that your lamp may go out and leave you permanently in the dark. While one is in this state, lo and behold, along comes the Lord of Truth with the oil of His providence to fuel your lamp. Your light is within your knowledge. [To quote two sayings of the Prophet (Allāh bless him and give him peace):]

> If someone puts into practice the knowledge he has already acquired, Allāh will endow him with knowledge of what he does not know.

> If someone devotes himself sincerely *[akhlaṣa]* to Allāh for forty mornings, the fountains of wisdom *[ḥikma]* will gush forth from his heart onto his tongue.

While he is in this state, he will suddenly see the fire of the Lord of Truth (Almighty and Glorious is He). Just like Moses (peace be upon him) at the moment when he saw a fire, he will say to his household:

> Stay here awhile. I notice a fire. (28:29)

The Lord of Truth will summon him by means of His fire. He will cause the fire to represent His nearness, and He will cause his vision of it to be his guide. When he sees a fire burning in the bush of his heart, he will say [to his household]: "Stay here awhile, right where you are now. I notice a fire." The innermost being *[sirr]* will call out to the heart:

> I am indeed your Lord. (20:12)
>
> I am Allāh..., so worship Me. (20:14)

[In other words:] "Do not submit yourself to anyone but Me. Acknowledge Me and ignore all others. Become connected to Me and disconnected from everything apart from Me. Seek Me and turn away from all others, toward My knowledge *['ilm]*, toward My nearness, toward My kingdom, toward My dominion."

When you experience this completely, the meeting will finally take place. Whatever is meant to happen will happen.

> And He revealed to His servant that which He revealed. (53:10)

The veils will be removed. Trouble and confusion will disappear. The lower self *[nafs]* will become calm. Peace *[sukūn]* will arrive. The gifts of grace *[alṭāf]* will arrive.

> Go to Pharaoh! (20:24)

"O heart, you must go back to the devil *[shaiṭān]*, the lower self *[nafs]* and the passions *[hawā]*. Set them on the path to Me. Guide them to Me. Say to them:

> O my people! Follow me. I will guide you to the way of right conduct. (40:38)

Become connected, then become disconnected, then become connected, then make connections *[ittaṣil thumma 'nqaṭi' thumma 'ttaṣil thumma awṣil]*.

As for you, O miserable wretch, your strength and energy will soon run out and leave you in the lurch. Your bosom friends will have nothing more to do with you. You will experience the combination of poverty in this world and punishment in the hereafter. The grave will come and squeeze you so tight that one set of ribs is crushed against the other, rendering you incapable of responding to the questions posed by [the two interrogating angels] *Munkar* and *Nakīr*. You will suffer agony in your grave, then a doorway to the Fire [of Hell] will be opened up for you, to let you be exposed to its torment and its toxic fumes.

O people of ours! Conduct yourselves properly in this abode [of the present life], so that your religion *[dīn]*, your outer *[ẓāhir]* and your inner *[bāṭin]* may be kept safe and sound until you are made to stand before Him at the Resurrection. When that moment comes, the veil will be removed from your eyes, from your mouth and from your ears, and He will feed you and make you grow from strength to strength, from insight to insight, from life to life, from perpetuity to perpetuity, from blessing to blessing. He will commend your hard work and praise your good conduct. He will call you grateful *[shākir]* after He has called you patient *[ṣābir]*, sensible *['āqil]* and devout *[dayyin]*. He will cause you to experience further transformation.

> Allāh does not change what is in a people, until they change what is in themselves. (13:11)

Bad character is something they must change by following the sacred law *[shar']*, then knowledge *['ilm]*, then the decree of destiny *[qadar]*.

It is as if they had been anesthetized *[bunnijū]* in readiness for the amputation of their hands and feet, for the amputation of their rotten, gangrenous limbs. There is no movement, no asking about the whys and wherefores. All consciousness, all human consciousness is lost, until the days of anesthesia *[tabannuj]* are over and consciousness returns to them. Then come the gracious favors of their Lord, to bring about transformation and further transformation. There is food to eat after hunger, something to drink after thirst, clothing to wear after nakedness.

As long as you are still following the path, He will command you to make do with very little, so that your carnal appetite *[shahwa]* may lose its intensity. You must give this ruling *[ḥukm]* its due, as you must be careful to observe all the commandments and prohibitions of the sacred law *[shar']*.

These days will come to an end, and your steps will draw near to the Lord of Truth (Almighty and Glorious is He) with the passing of the night and the coming of the day. They [meaning people who follow the spiritual path] are grouped in various categories: There are some for whom the entire journey takes only a day, while for others it may take a month or even several years. Instead of wasting your time on the whys and the wherefores and on speculating about the future, you should pull yourself together, get moving and get down to work.

If you labor in His palace, perhaps He will take you on as a permanent member of the staff. Maybe one of His slave girls will fall in love with you and you will marry her. Your outward appearance will be transformed. [Those laborer's tools of yours,] your basket made of palm leaves and your hoe can be sold off. You will be installed as a manager, a royal deputy and minister *[wazīr]*. When someone really knows *['arafa]* Allāh, he does not regard such things as being too much to ask of Him. Once you have attained to Him, He will whet your appetite. Abstinence and renunciation are appropriate before direct experience *[ma'rifa]*, before you attain to the King, before you know who you really are *[qabla an ta'rifa man anta]*, what your title *[laqab]* is and what your name *[ism]* is.

The servant says goodbye to his worldly goods, to his clothes, his furniture, his home, his family, his children, his neighbors, his wife and his closest friends. He puts one foot forward and drags the other. With two steps, fear and hope, he moves away from the past.

Nothing is familiar to him, for he is leaving everything behind, not knowing what he can expect or what may be expected of him. Then, once he has left everything behind, he arrives at the door of the King. There he stands in the company of His attendants, along with His riding animals, feeling both fear and hope, not knowing what may be in store for him. Meanwhile the King, who is watching him and has been informed about him, says to the attendants: "Give him special treatment, ahead of all the rest!" Then he gets to be employed in one post after another, until he is installed as a chamberlain *[ḥājib]* in His presence, as a special confidant who is privy to His secrets, invested with a robe of honor, with neckband, waistband and crown. Now he can write to tell his family:

> Come to me with all your folk. (12:93)

After the King has called Himself as witness to His promise: "I shall not change toward you," he has a guarantee of constant companionship and friendship *[wilāya]*, since abstinence *[zuhd]* cannot coexist with intimate knowledge *[ma'rifa]*.

A case like this is one in a million. This is something that comes about as a result of divine destiny *[qadar]*, preordainment *[sābiqa]* and foreknowledge *['ilm]*.

Do not be one of those concerning whom Allāh has said:

> No, I swear by the censorious self *[bi'n-nafsi'l-lawwāma]*. (75:2)

The believer *[mu'min]* must ask, as a way of calling himself to account and improving his behavior: "What did I intend by saying what I said? What did I intend by taking the step I took? What did I intend by eating what I ate? Why did I act as I did? Why did I do it? Is this in accordance with the Book and the Sunna?"

You must acquire certitude *[yaqīn]* after self-examination *[muḥāsaba]*, for it is the kernel *[lubb]* of faith *[īmān]*. Only with certitude can the obligatory religious duties *[farā'iḍ]* be properly discharged. Only with certitude can one put this world in its proper place.

When you receive a response to your supplication *[du'ā']*, calm and composure, but if your prayer *[da'wa]* is not answered, you get upset!

One of the distinguishing features of the champions of truth *[ṣiddīqūn]* is that they resort to Allāh in every case. When they wish to conceal their spiritual states *[aḥwāl]*, they may resort to the give and take of dealing with creatures, but their hearts remain with Him while their bodies are in the company of His creatures. The human being *[ibn Ādam]* needs to work in this world, in order to transform his natural tendencies *[ṭab']*. He must struggle against his lower self *[nafs]*, his devil *[shaiṭān]* and his passions *[hawā]*, in order to move beyond the attributes of the animals *[ṣifāt al-bahā'im]* and acquire human characteristics *[akhlāq insāniyya]*.

Do you disbelieve *[kafarta]* in this Lord,

> Who created you from dust, then from a sperm, then shaped you as a man? (18:37)

Does He deserve as His recompense that you should deny Him and repudiate Him, that you should feel embarrassed to be seen by the eyes of other people, yet feel no sense of shame before Him, although He can always see you?

O you who make no secret of your claim to saintship *[wilāya]*, while committing blatant sins of disobedience against the Lord of Truth! Do you feel no sense of shame before Him, when He is well aware of your innermost being *[sirr]* and your conscience *[sarīra]*? And you there, you who make a display of poverty while concealing your wealth, are you not ashamed to be trading your religion *[dīn]* for your worldly interests?

> Whatever blessing you enjoy, it is from Allāh. (16:53)

Where is your gratitude?

O young man! Do not accuse anyone on behalf of your Creator. You are just as likely to be mistaken as you are to be correct [in what you suspect about another person]. Do not present other people in a bad light, in order to have Him approve of your own conduct. It is up to the sacred law *[shar']*, not our own minds, to determine whether a favorable or an unfavorable view should be taken. This is in relation to the outer *[ẓāhir]*. You must also be careful to recognize cases where it is up to the inner *[bāṭin]* to determine whether something merits disapproval or approval. The verdict *[fatwā]* of the heart can overrule the verdict of the jurist *[faqīh]*, because the jurist arrives at his verdict through some exercise of his *ijtihād*,[20] whereas the heart always bases its judgment on what is strictly correct *['azīma]*, on that which is pleasing to the Lord of Truth and in compliance with His wishes. This is the judgment *[qaḍā']* of knowledge *['ilm]* over the legal ruling *[ḥukm]*.

You must be servants of the law *[ḥukm]*, then servants of knowledge *['ilm]* while remaining in servitude to the law, in the sense that you must conform to it in humble compliance. You must enter along with knowledge into the company of the law. Any "matter of fact" *[ḥaqīqa]* that is not acknowledged by the sacred law *[sharī'a]* is an atheistic heresy *[zandaqa]*.

When you enter into the company of the people of the Lord of Truth (Almighty and Glorious is He), you will experience what they experience and share the food they eat.

You must express your gratitude to Allāh (Exalted is He) in secret and in private.

O people of this city, everything you are involved in is repugnant in my sight, just as everything I am involved in is repugnant in your eyes. We are opposites that cannot be reconciled. We manage to live amongst you thanks to the power of the Owner of the heavens, but there is no no permanent residence here for the joy of our hearts.

Your youth has been spent in ways displeasing to the Creator (Almighty and Glorious is He). You are eager to please your wife, your children, your neighbor and your worldly ruler *[sulṭān]*, yet you earn the displeasure of the angels *[malā'ika]* and the Lord of Truth (Almighty and Glorious is He), although:

[20] As a technical term of Islāmic jurisprudence, *ijtihād* means the effort made by a qualified expert to reach an independent judgment on a point of law, through the interpretation and application of the four basic sources or principles *[uṣūl]*, namely the Qur'ān, the Sunna, the consensus *[ijmā']* of the recognized authorities, and deduction by analogy *[qiyās]*.

> ...unto Him is the homeward journey *[ilaihi'l-maṣīr].* (5:18)

You are bound to answer the call of death. You will meet up with your fathers and mothers, brethren, friends and rulers. Let none of you ask: "When will the Resurrection take place?" For when you die you will experience your own Resurrection *[qiyāma].*

The saints *[awliyā']* of Allāh (Almighty and Glorious is He) are already there in the nearness of the Lord of Truth (Almighty and Glorious is He). They have lived their lives in a close relationship with the Lord of Truth. They have died many deaths: first of all to that which is unlawful *[ḥarām]*, secondly to that which is dubious *[shubha]*, thirdly to that which is indifferently permissible *[mubāḥ]*, fourthly to that which is unambiguously lawful *[ḥalāl ṭilq]*, and fifthly to everything apart from Allāh (Almighty and Glorious is He). They are dead to all these things; they neither seek them nor come anywhere near them. They appear to have undergone a transmutation, turning them into inner contents *[ma'ānī]* with no outer forms *[ṣuwar].* Then Allāh (Exalted is He) revives them.

> In the Name of Allāh shall be its course and its mooring. (11:41)

When hearts are following a course that takes them across the oceans of destiny *[qadar]*, their mooring is at the door of His knowledge *['ilm]* and His nearness.

Wakefulness is a form of service, while sleep is a means of connection *[wuṣla].* When the servant falls asleep during a ritual prayer *[ṣalāt]*, Allāh displays him proudly to His angels. The physical body is a cage and the spirit *[rūḥ]* is a bird.

In the eyes of the people of real experience *[ma'rifa]*, creatures are like flies and hornets, or like silkworms. Their spiritual states *[aḥwāl]* have no relevance for you.

Be sensible! No one but a stupid fool would bring destruction upon himself to spite Allāh; no one would do such a thing unless he was doomed to destruction anyway.

If someone tells you to be generous in spending and giving, that person is your friend. If someone gets rich on what belongs to the poor, he will be reduced to poverty because of it.

More is required of you than merely professing Islām. When will you put the truth into practice? When will you act on the truth?

When my limbs move, you should realize that my heart is aflame.

> O world here below *[yā dunyā]*, taste bitter to My saints *[awliyā']* at the outset, so that they will not love you, but serve them later on, so that they will not be preoccupied with you.

When the Hour [of Resurrection] was mentioned in the hearing of Mary's son Jesus (peace be upon him), he would wail like a woman bereaved of her child, saying: "It is not fitting for the son of Adam to stay calm when the Hour *[as-sā'a]* is mentioned in his hearing." You are a nonentity. You have no feeling in you. You have never loved or been loved. He grieved over the length of his sojourn in this world, because it made him afraid of the fickleness of human beings, dependence on creatures, and separation from the All-Merciful *[ar-Raḥmān]* because of the dominating influence of the passions *[hawā]*, the lower self *[nafs]*, the natural impulses *[ṭab']* and the devil *[shaiṭān]*. Anyone who feels secure in this world must be mightily ignorant indeed.

O young man! I am reassured, whatever may happen. I am made to feel afraid, whatever may happen. By my life, He draws you near and brings you close, He speaks to you, He feeds you and nourishes you, He watches over you, He opens doors for you, He seats you at the table of His gracious favor and His nearness, He puts you at your ease, but He still requires you to experience grief.

A man approached him to ask him something, but he would not listen to him. The Shaikh went on to say:

This is the place of grief. There comes a flash of lightning and soon abundant rain will pour down all around. The servant tries to get close to the Lord of Truth (Almighty and Glorious is He), but nearness is attained only after mastery of the law *[iḥkām al-ḥukm]*, after the book of certainty *[yaqīn]* has been made available to him and he has learned its secrets and what is to become of him.

The brother of Ibn 'Aqīl was an expert in Qur'ānic readings *[qirā'āt]* and Islamic jurisprudence *[fiqh]*, but when he was seen in the land of the infidels *[kuffār]*, wearing a crucifix *[ṣalīb]* around his neck, he was asked: "What have you done with those readings of the Qur'ān and all that pious devotion?" To which he replied: "I know nothing of the Qur'ān apart from one single verse *[āya]*:

> And We shall advance upon the work they have done, and make it into scattered particles of dust. (25:23)

The first to be guilty of apostasy is the innermost being *[sirr]*, then the heart *[qalb]*, then the self *[nafs]*, then the limbs and organs of the physical body *[jawāriḥ]*. When the innermost being apostasizes *[irtadda]*, it is bound to become apparent [that it has deserted the faith].

The hypocrite *[munāfiq]* in the mosque *[masjid]* is like a bird in a cage. The outer framework of the sacred law *[ẓāhir ash-shar']* is his cage. If we were at liberty to treat knowledge *['ilm]* as the outer framework, we would publicize your sins on your behalf. We would say: "O unbeliever *[yā kāfir]*! O sinner *[yā fāsiq]*!" But the sacred law has tied our hands, so this we cannot do.

You must observe the rules *[ḥukm]*. You must also seek knowledge *['ilm]*, because knowledge will uncover the truth for you. Study the sacred law, then you may retire [to concentrate on your private devotions]. If you are one of His special few *[khawāṣṣ]*, He will instruct you in His knowledge.

When the self *[nafs]* has finally brought you to its Master *[Mawlā]*, it will stop at the door while you make the kind of entrance made by kings. When you see that the door is open, you will be told: "You may not enter just as you are. You have an obligation to your kinsfolk."

> And come to me with all your folk. (12:93)

"O innermost *[yā sirr]*, you must stick together with your heart, your physical body and your entire being."

At this point there will be no buying, no selling and no bartering.

Eat, O you who have not eaten! Drink, O you who have not drunk!

When the well has endured the digging and the instruments of excavation, the water finally springs from it. It becomes a place of refuge for the weary wanderer and the thirsty traveler. If you do not endure with patience the agonies of constant struggle and affliction, when will you ever be someone who really knows *['ārif]*? O patient pauper *[faqīr ṣābir]*, very soon now the Lord of Truth will look on you with favor. He will raise you up. He will crown you and invest you with the robes of might and dominion and majesty.

O Allāh, from them [from creatures]—remoteness, and to You—nearness! O Allāh, from them—independence, and of You—dire need!

Make sure of keeping Allāh, by doing without everything apart from Him!

While your heart is clinging to the door of His nearness, but is still immersed in the darkness of worldly existence *[wujūd]*, the first light of knowledge *['ilm]* will suddenly dawn upon it. The eyes of your heart will be soothed with the ointment of the innermost being *[sirr]*, and you will read the index of the the decrees of destiny *[aqdār]*. Then you will discover that food and drink await you beyond the entrance to the Garden [of Paradise], carefully selected for the kings of His creatures and the nobles among His saints *[awliyā']*. You will eat and drink. You will enjoy a long sleep without tossing and turning. You will say: "I am one of the saints *[awliyā']* of Allāh. I am one of the abdāl. This is not just a daydream."

The noblest of Allāh's creatures are ever attentive to the wishes of Allāh. Have you any idea what this could mean, you people who like to go to meetings *[ahl al-majālis]*, you born gossips?

The Shaikh blew into his hand, and turned his face in all directions.

If someone claims to love Allāh (Almighty and Glorious is He), yet does not practice self-control *[wara']* in his private life, that person must be a liar. If someone claims to love the Garden [of

Paradise], yet does not use his money and his property for charitable purposes, that person must be a liar. If someone claims to love the Prophet (Allāh bless him and give him peace), yet has no love for poverty and the poor, that person must be a liar.

With the eye of the head *['ain ar-ra's]* you witness this world, with the eye of the heart *['ain al-qalb]* you witness the hereafter, and with the eye of the innermost being *['ain as-sirr]* you witness the Master *[Mawlā]*.

You behave so politely in the company of fellow creatures, minding your manners by not raising your voice above that of someone else, yet you defy the Lord of Truth (Almighty and Glorious is He) with sinful disobedience and try to outdo Him in His actions. Shame on you!

The rising sun would only have ignorant fools to shine upon, if no one put Allāh before his own passions *[hawā]*, his natural impulses *[ṭab']* and his lower self *[nafs]*. This is something that surpasses ordinary understanding.

You may influence the spirit *[rūḥ]* and the natural disposition *[ṭab']* through gentle persuasion and accommodation, but not by compulsion.

> ...excepting one who has been compelled [to declare himself an unbeliever], while his heart is still content with faith. (16:106)

Whenever the honest disciple *[murīd ṣādiq]* is approached by a newcomer, he holds the person's outer conduct *[a'māl ẓāhira]* up to the mirror of the law *[ḥukm]*, while reviewing his inner conduct *[a'māl bāṭina]* in the mirror of knowledge *['ilm]*. Then, if his actions appear correct in both mirrors, he admits him to the presence of the King (Almighty and Glorious is He). If an action fits one mirror and not the other, however, he will not be allowed to enter. He must sit at the door, where he will be told: "You must strive to become proficient in your business, to the point where your efforts deserve commendation and the state of your affairs is worthy of praise. This door can only be entered through the door of the law *[ḥukm]* and knowledge *['ilm]*. When approached accordingly, it will be opened for you."

Certain actions belong in a separate category. These actions are a secret between you and your Lord (Almighty and Glorious is He). This kind of action is recognized neither by any favored angel *[malak muqarrab]* nor by any Messenger-Prophet *[nabī mursal]*.

[Certain servants of the Lord] are deprived of their legalistic intellects *['uqūl shar'iyya]* and are endowed with the intellect of intellects *['aql al-'uqūl]*, until, when their days of anesthesia *[tabannuj]* are over, they are restored to food after hunger, drink after thirst, sleep after insomnia and relaxation after exhaustion. Then the servant is sent back to do a job of work. Since he has become acquainted with the treasure houses of the [divine] mysteries, this servant must now learn how he needs to be in relation to the people of his town and region. If he is the *Quṭb* [spiritual pole, pivot or axis], he is aware of the doings of all the people of this world, of their allotted portions *[aqsām]* and how their affairs will ultimately work out. He is also familiar with the treasure houses of the [divine] mysteries, and nothing in this world is hidden from him, be it good or bad, because he has been singled out by the King as His confidential servant *[biṭāna]*, as the deputy *[nā'ib]* of His Prophets *[anbiyā']* and His Messengers *[rusul]*, as the custodian of the Kingdom *[amīn al-mamlaka]*. Such is this very special individual *['ain]*, the *Quṭb* in his own era.

The heart is the resort *[mawrid]* of the angels *[malā'ika]*, while the innermost being *[sirr]* beholds the Lord of Truth (Almighty and Glorious is He).

When Allāh wishes to have a servant become devoted to Him entirely, the first step He takes is to alienate him from human beings *[banī Ādam]*. Then He causes him to feel at home in the company of savage beasts, wild animals and the jinn. In due course, when he has lost his human loneliness through familiarity with the jinn and the creatures of the wild, He introduces him to the angels in all their different forms. In the desert wastes and in the oceans he hears their speech: "O you who are committed to total dedication, listen well! O seeker of the Lord of Truth (Almighty and Glorious is He), [first you must hear] the spoken word, then [your eyes will see] the vision." Then, when he has grown accustomed to their speech and is yearning to see their shapes and forms, the veil between him and them is finally removed. Among all the creatures of Allāh, none have a more delightful way of speaking than the angels. Of all created beings they are the most beautiful in form and the most pleasant in speech.

At this point a veil is drawn again, and He transports the servant to His door. Then He lets him enjoy the intimacy *[uns]* of His nearness. Then whatever is meant to be, will be.

After a period of silence, He sends inspiration *[yūḥī]* to the heart, just as He sent inspiration to the mother of Moses (peace be upon him) when she was fearing for his safety: "O heart, if you are afraid for the safety of the innermost being *[sirr]* within you, cast the physical body adrift in the ocean of the wastelands and deserts, and say goodbye to family and friends. A woman better than you would cast her son upon the open sea, while you are afraid of taking a couple of steps forward. This is because of your lack of faith *[īmān]*.

> If We had not fortified her heart... (28:10)

In your own case, therefore, when you are afraid of losing your pious devotion *[birr]* during the time of separation from both the object of your quest and your familiar environment, so that you are on the point of resorting once again to creatures and material means *[sabab]*, it is at this very moment that He will fortify your heart.

O you who are so lacking in realization of the Divine Unity *[tawḥīd]*, in knowledge *['ilm]* and dutiful devotion *[taqwā]*, how far you are from practicing repentance in every situation! O backslider, to make a living by exploiting religion *[dīn]* is hypocrisy *[nifāq]*, while to live by working at a trade or profession is accordance with the Sunna. You must continue to follow this recommended practice, until faith *[īmān]* arrives. You must take your skill in hand and shut creatures out of your heart. Then, whether you leave home or stay there, you will function within the abode of His knowledge. Blind and deaf, you will hear no one other than the Lord of Truth, and you will see nothing but the gracious bounty of the Lord of

Truth. Then you will go on a journey, traveling to every corner of the earth in the company of the Chief Inspector *[shiḥna]*. O common folk *['awāmm]*, not one of you will go abroad and travel, even when you have the opportunity!

[It may seem to be] the case that one receives from creatures, when in actual fact *[ḥaqīqa]* it is a case of receiving from the Lord of Truth (Almighty and Glorious is He). As for someone who has progressed to an advanced stage of development, and whose saintship *[wilāya]* has been confirmed, it would never occur to his heart to receive without giving. Things just come to him, even though he is indifferent to them, simply because he is destined to receive them.

O mother of Moses, if you are afraid for his safety, cast him upon the open sea! You too, if you fear for your religion *[dīn]*, cast your heart upon Allāh! Commit your heart to His safekeeping. Commit your family to His safekeeping. Say: "You shall be the Companion on my journey and the Custodian of my wife and children!"

Your intimate knowledge *[ma'rifa]* of Allāh (Almighty and Glorious is He) and your love *[maḥabba]* for Him are like a sash *[himyān]* around your waist, which stays with you whichever way you turn, so you can sleep in the company of destiny *[qadar]* and take instruction from the Power *[qudra]* and the All-Powerful One *[al-Qādir]*.

By Allāh, and then again by Allāh! The spiritual states *[aḥwāl]* of the saints *[awliyā']* are like the spiritual states of the Prophets *[anbiyā']*, although their title *[laqab]* is different from their titles *[alqāb]*. The Prophets and Messengers *[mursalūn]* are not visited in their graves by [the interrogating angels] *Munkar* and *Nakīr*, because they are the intercessors *[shufa'ā']* on behalf of creatures. Thus they will not be called to account [at the Resurrection], because they are the élite *[khawāṣṣ]* of all creation.

O slave of the passions *[hawā]* and natural urges *[ṭab']*! O slave of commendation and praise! You must inevitably receive your full quota of the allotments on [the recording of] which the pen [of destiny] has run dry, and of which there has been [divine] foreknowledge from time immemorial *[sabaqa bihi'l-'ilm]*. The important question, however, is whether you will receive them through you or through Him.

Will you assert your own existence, or will you annihilate you with the affirmation of Divine Unity *[tawḥīd]*? A secret of the Lord of Truth (Almighty and Glorious is He) within the heart of His servant is inaccessible to the devil *[shaiṭān]*, to human minds *['uqūl]* and to the angel *[malak]*. Seek nearness [to Him] through the door of your nonexistence *[fanā']*. If you are content, He will love you, and when He loves you, He will teach you [His secrets]. He will make you His companion. You will always be in His company with your knowledge *['ilm]*, as the devout worshipper *['ābid]* enjoys His company through his worshipful service *['ibāda]*.

Only someone with real experience *['ārif]* can know that this is what it means to be a disciple *[murīd]*. You are subject to his direction, so if you comply with the wishes of Allāh in this respect, [all will be well]; otherwise you will be treated as an outcast. We used to trail along behind such people, as if we were no more than specks of dust, in order to learn the passwords *[kalimāt ad-dukhūl]* from them. To rely entirely on one's own subjective opinion *[ra'y]* is to go astray.

After some discussion, the Shaikh (may Allāh be well pleased with him) went on to say:

He is the deputy *[nā'ib]* of the Messenger *[rasūl]*. As far as following him is concerned, when he leaves something alone, it should be left alone. When he accepts something, it should be accepted. He leaves alone what should be left alone, and he accepts what should be accepted. He sheds light on the matter for you, like the break of dawn *[ṣubḥ]*. He gives the servant two new sets of clothes, sometimes those of existence *[wujūd]* and sometimes those of nonexistence *[fanā']*. There will be times when he is caused to be absent, while the Lord of Truth holds his attention, and times when he is caused to be present, in order to convey information from the Lord of Truth: "My heart has related, on the authority of my Lord *[rawā qalbī 'an Rabbī]*..."

You must provide two doors for your private retreat: a door leading to creatures and a door leading to the Lord of Truth. You must observe the rights of creatures *[ḥuqūq al-khalq]*, and you must also observe the rights of the Truth *[ḥuqūq al-Ḥaqq]*. Make friends with creatures for the sake of the Lord of Truth, then you will be safe from the evil of creatures and will always enjoy the company of the Lord of Truth. Creatures are everything apart from the Lord of Truth, and this statement is meant to be of universal application. By saying that you should make friends with creatures, we mean that you should offer them good advice *[naṣīḥa]*. After befriending the Lord of Truth, then is the time to make friends with creatures. If you make friends with creatures only after securing the friendship of the Lord of Truth, then you will be attached to Him and not to His creatures. The distinguishing feature of your friendship with creatures should be that you do not regard them as the source of benefit or harm, but keep them all under control and subject to your direction.

[There are those who have] hearts that have tasted the food of His gracious favor, heard His conversation and experienced the joy of His nearness. Allāh has spoken directly to their hearts, here in this world before death. All will be addressed [by Him] at the Resurrection *[qiyāma]*, but only a very few individuals are so addressed in this world.

Abū'l-Qāsim al-Junaid once said: "I have never made a pronouncement without the testimony of forty of the *Abdāl*, one of their number being Sarī as-Saqaṭī."[21] Nor would he put their words into practice until he had seen a vision of the Messenger (Allāh bless him and give him peace), saying to him: "O Junaid, speak to the people, for the moment when you must speak has now arrived."

[21] See notes [4, 5] and [10] above.

If you seek to be worthy of the Lord of Truth, to develop and make steady progress, you must practice what you preach; otherwise, woe unto you!

When performing the prayer *[ṣalāt]*, you turn to face the *qibla* [direction of the Ka'ba, the Sanctuary in Mecca]. When suffering misfortune, there is also a *qibla* you should face. That is to say, you should turn the face of your heart toward the Lord of Truth (Almighty and Glorious is He), just as you would turn your outer face toward the Ka'ba. If you turn your face toward creatures in times of adversity, your faith *[īmān]* must be false, because the suffering ought to subside in the presence of faith. For hearts to break because of misfortune is a major sin *[kabīra]*. The hearts of ordinary people get broken over things of this world. With the élite *[khawāṣṣ]* it is over [the loss] of some otherworldly pleasure. As for the élite of the élite *[khawāṣṣ al-khawāṣṣ]*, their hearts get broken over losing contact with the Master *[Mawlā]*, or because a veil descends after insight had been granted. Each group experiences its own particular form of heartbreak, but few indeed are those exceptional individuals whose heartbreak is for the sake of the Lord of Truth (Almighty and Glorious is He).

Someone asked him about the saying of the Prophet (Allāh bless him and give him peace) :

> Allāh does not accept a supplication *[du'ā']* that is phrased like a crude jingle *[malḥūn]*.

He explained:

Allāh does not accept a supplication that is couched artificially in rhymed prose *[musajja']*. [As the Prophet (Allāh bless him and give him peace) also said:]

> I and the dutifully devoted members *[atqiyā']* of my community *[umma]* are free from affectation *[takalluf]*.

The believer *[mu'min]* may sometimes experience an overwhelming feeling of high hope. He examines the register *[dīwān]* of his sins and does not find a single sin recorded there. He has been trained along the right lines *[rushd]* ever since his early childhood, from [basic religious studies in] elementary school *[kuttāb]*, to [learning to become] a reciter of the Qur'ān *[muqri']*, to [leading the communal prayers as Imām in] a prayer niche *[miḥrāb]*. This may indeed happen, although such a case would be very unusual. Here we have someone against whom no sinful disobedience has been listed, while the register of commandments *[dīwān al-awāmir]* records no instruction that he has failed to carry out. He will therefore be condemned to commit an act of disobedience *[ma'ṣiya]* of some kind, so that he may not perish. Then he must make amends and repent. This act of disobedience will thus be his preordained lot *[sābiqa]*, like the birthmark on his head. This sin, in relation to this believer and champion of the truth *[ṣiddīq]*, is like the sin of Adam (peace be upon him). This is most unusual, however, and it is so extraordinary that we need not dwell on it or attach any importance to it.

The will power *[irāda]* within the self *[nafs]* is actually two different wills: the will of that which is apart from the Lord of Truth, and the will of the Lord of Truth Himself. These two are engaged in a process of reconciliation and conflict until a person reaches the age of forty. This is the significance of the saying of the Prophet (Allāh bless him and give him peace):

> If someone reaches the age of forty, and the good in him has not gained the upper hand over the bad in him, then he may as well get ready for the Fire [of Hell].

[This is] an allusion to the principle just mentioned.

O you who reject the clear explanation *[bayān]* of the spiritual paths *[ṭuruq]*! The outer *[ẓāhir]* is a wet nurse *[ẓi'r]*. The vision of the inner *[bāṭin]* is a weaning *[infiṭām]*.

As long as you acknowledge all apart from Him, and they acknowledge you, you are in a state of delusion.

Sometimes you must follow them [the spiritual guides], and sometimes you must humble yourself before them. This house has two paths leading to it.

The mark of the saint *[walī]* is dependence on Allāh for everything, satisfaction with Allāh instead of everything, and consultation with Allāh about everything. If your lower self *[nafs]* will insist on laying claim to saintship *[wilāya]*, you must therefore keep it in line with these qualities. If it does not conform, you are no saint.

It is not appropriate for the learned scholar *['ālim]* to enter the presence of kings until after his faith *[īmān]* and his dutiful devotion *[ittiqā']* are thoroughly confirmed, his knowledge *['ilm]* of Allāh and his pious abstinence *[zuhd]* are strongly established, and he is firmly rooted in real experience *[ma'rifa]* and intimate friendship *[uns]* with Allāh. Then he can enter their presence in full strength, and he can also leave their presence in full strength.

I once kept company with a certain person who could tell me what had already happened to me and what was going to happen to me. A handsome young man used to go around with him, and he would visit the people in power *[salāṭīn]*. Something about this made me feel uneasy *[khaṭara bi-qalbī]*, but he said to me: "O my son, this young man was in a hospice *[ribāṭ]* and I was afraid that, if I left him there, they would come to ruin because of him. As for my visiting the people in power, it is not that I have any need of them. I only visit them in order to preach to them and to show them the paths of justice *[ṭuruq al-'adl]*."

As for all of you, there are shortcomings in the way you behave in company [with the Shaikhs], whereas we observe good manners in their company.

Someone asked: "If the food is mixed, how can one's fasting *[ṣiyām]* and prayers *[ṣalāt]* be valid?" The Shaikh replied:

What is lawful *[ḥalāl]* is clear and what is unlawful *[ḥarām]* is clear. The sacred law *[shar']* makes it clear to you, as does pausing to check your feeling about it. If your heart tells you no, it is unlawful, and if your heart tells you yes, it is lawful. If it stays silent and says neither yes nor no, then it is something dubious *[shubha]*.

If everything to which you are accustomed has been taken away, yet your lower self *[nafs]* endures with patience, this is the state of contentment *[qanā'a]*.

You must realize that what is important is not how many acts of obedience, fasts and prayers you perform in His sight. All that He wants from you is a pure heart, free from troubles and others [apart from Him]. The hypocritical abstainer is pure and serene on the outside *[ẓāhir]*, but his inner *[bāṭin]* is full of murky confusion. There may be a palor in his cheeks, he may hold his shoulders in a humble attitude, and he may wear a garment of coarse wool *[ṣūf]*, but his abstinence is a matter of restraining his hands while his inner is begging. His lower self *[nafs]* is keenly affected by praise and blame. His eye is greedily watching the things other people possess.

As for the person with real experience *['ārif]*, his outer may be stained by some of the things allotted by destiny *[aqsām]*, things allotted to him personally and others that have become attached to him. As the King's expert *[jahbadh]*, he is like the superintendant *[ustādh]* of His palace, the commander of His army, and all the while he preserves the integrity of his innermost being *[sirr]*, the purity of his heart and access to His Majesty's presence. He is splashed by the waves of knowledge *['ilm]*, but the ocean of this world does not fill his heart. In relation to his heart, all that the seven heavens and earths contain, as well the rest of creation, is virtually nonexistent *[mutalāshiya]*. This is the description of one who really knows *['ārif]*, as that was the description of the pious abstainer *[zāhid]*. You do not have a clue about this, so why not hold your tongue instead of passing judgment on people?

O you who snatch this world from the hands of its owners *[arbāb]* by exploiting the hereafter! O you who are so ignorant of the Truth, you are more in need of repentance than these ordinary folk *['awāmm]*. Your obligation to confess your sins is far greater than theirs. You have nothing good, no profit *[ribḥ]* and no spirit *[rūḥ]*, no salvation *[najāt]* and no light *[nūr]*. You have no religion *[dīn]*, and as for this world *[dunyā]* of yours, it will not last. You grasp with your natural urges *[ṭibāʿ]* and your passions *[ahwiya]*; you grasp this world for its own sake, not for the sake of the hereafter. My business is with you. My words are directed at you. (He is saying all this with reference to the preachers *[wuʿʿāẓ]* of his own time and his own city.)

Turn a deaf ear [to distracting voices] and try to acquire knowledge. Let no one say a word. It is someone else's turn to speak. I am borrowing my tongue today. I am borrowing my outer frame *[qālab]* today. Intimate friendship is to be found in exile *[ghurba]*, and lonely isolation is the key to nearness [to the Lord]. O you who can be quiet in private, the important question now is whether you can also be quiet in public. O my dear son, first private life, then public life; dumbness, then verbal utterance; attention to the King *[malik]*, then attention to the King's slave *[mamlūk]*.

One of the champions of truth *[ṣiddīqūn]* has said that what is unambiguously lawful *[ḥalāl ṭilq]* is to be found among those who are spiritually developed *[rūḥāniyyūn]*. You must seek to become one of those who are spiritually developed, until your own spiritual state *[ḥāl]* coincides with theirs. You must be able to tell the difference between the bad and the good. The lamp of your innermost being *[sirr]* is the sun of your intimate knowledge *[maʿrifa]*, the moon of your nearness to your Lord. That which is unlawful *[ḥarām]* is coexistent with your lower self *[nafs]*, that which is dubious *[shubha]* is coexistent with the heart *[qalb]*, and that which is unambiguously lawful *[ḥalāl ṭilq]* is coexistent with purity of the innermost being *[sirr]*. This is beyond all powers of mental comprehension *[ʿuqūl]*. As long as a lower self is still there, you will eat unlawful food. As long as a heart is still there, you will eat dubious food. But if an innermost being is there in a state of purity, then you will eat food that is unquestionably lawful.

The Shaikh said: Why? It has been said:

> Surely the self *[nafs]* is always inciting *[ammāra]* to evil. (12:53)

You do not care where your food comes from, like the bad wife who says to her husband: "Steal and get me something to eat!" She cannot tell the difference between what is lawful and what is unlawful.

This is why the Prophet (Allāh bless him and give him peace) has said:

> Find a religious woman *[dhāt ad-dīn]* to marry. Let your hands be filled with dust!

A religious woman will assist you in matters pertaining to your life hereafter. The self *[nafs]* is like this wife, because inwardly *[bāṭinan]* it wishes to distinguish between what is lawful and what is unlawful.

When something apparently quite lawful is right there in front of you, even if it is part of your own earnings, you must pause to consider. Suppose that it had not been baked or cooked, [what about the ingredients?] Then let your heart refer to your innermost being *[sirr]*, and let your innermost being refer to your Lord (Almighty and Glorious is He). The Lord of Truth (Almighty and Glorious is He) will send an angel *[malak]* to your heart, and if the food is lawful he will tell you:

> Eat of the good things with which We have provided you... (2:172)[22]

The angel will recite the whole of this Qur'ānic verse *[āya]* to your heart, whereupon you may eat. But if it should happen to be something unlawful or dubious, he will say to you:

> And do not eat of that over which the Name of Allāh has not been mentioned. (6:121)

Such food is unlawful, so do not go near it, because Allāh will give you something better in exchange for it. You must sit and wait for His judgment *[qaḍā']* and His decree *[qadar]*, in obedient submission *[mustasliman]* until the hand of His gracious favor is extended to you. Then you must reach out with your own hand to accept your full quota of the shares allotted to you.

[22] The rest of the verse reads: "and give thanks to Allāh if you truly worship Him alone."

Abstinence *[zuhd]* is the work of an hour and cautious restraint *[wara']* is the work of two hours, but real experience *[ma'rifa]* is the work of eternity.

If we compare your spiritual states *[aḥwāl]* with the spiritual states of your predecessors, we do not find you matching up to them in any respect at all. You have obeyed your own lower self *[nafs]*, so it has come to look down on you. You have satisfied its carnal desires, so it has adopted an arrogant attitude toward you. If only you had cut its lines of supply! You might have tried to defeat it, but you chose instead to provide it with everything it desired. You opened a door for your devil *[shaiṭān]*, because it is he who instills craving in the lower self. It has no language, but the devil of the jinn knows how to reach it, although the devil of humankind is the only one who can actually make you do something. When it gets indigestion from over-indulgence, if it is put on a diet and you wean it from things that are unlawful *[ḥarām]*, dubious *[shubuhāt]* or ambiguous *[mutashabbihāt]*, its excitement will calm down. If you would reduce its intake of permissible food *[mubāḥ]*, it would become less prone to excessive indulgence. Its cravings would be uprooted from it, and the trees of fear and hope would grow in it instead. Light would be shed on the darkness of its inner being *[bāṭin]*. It would come to be at peace with its heart. Then it would hear a voice calling out to it:

> O self now at peace *[yā ayyatuha'n-nafsu'l-muṭma'inna]*, return unto your Lord, well pleased, well pleasing! (89:27)

The common man *['āmmī]* will hear it calling to him at the moment of death: "How far away you are from the banquet of nearness, from the chamber of the [Lord's] presence!"

> And in Our sight they [Our purified servants] are indeed among the chosen ones, the excellent. (38:47)

Your heart *[qalb]* will not be pure until your lower self *[nafs]* comes to be like the dog *[kalb]* of the Companions of the Cave *[aṣḥāb al-kahf]*, a faithful follower keeping watch at the threshold of nearness [to the Lord]. The heart is in His presence, while the servant waits for it to re-emerge.

You must observe the external requirements of the sacred law *[ẓāhir ash-sharʿ]* as long as your faith *[īmān]* is still weak. You may take advantage of special concessions *[rukhṣa]* in accordance with the Book and the Sunna. Then, once your faith has grown strong, you must learn to ride the strict ruling *[ʿazīma]* and the most rigorous interpretation. If you use your own lower self *[nafs]* as a vehicle, you can travel along with destiny *[qadar]* and keep pace with it as you go.

Someone said to al-Ḥallāj when he was being crucified: "Give me a piece of good advice!" He responded to this by saying: "[My advice concerns] your lower self *[nafs]*. If you can control it, [well and good] otherwise it will control you."

I once owned a shirt, back at the outset of my career. It was a very nice one. I offered it for sale in the market on numerous occasions, but no one would buy it. Then I approached a certain person and left it in pawn with him for one dīnār—until the religious holidays *[ayyām al-ʿīd]* came around, when who should turn up but that man with the shirt! "Take it and wear it," said he, "and you need not feel obliged to repay the dīnār." I was reluctant to accept, but he said: "Take it, otherwise I shall burn it!" So he gave me no choice but to wear it. At this point I realized that it was my allotted portion *[qism]*, from which I had no right to abstain.

The Shaikh was asked about the saying of one of the scholars: "We tried to acquire knowledge *[ʿilm]* other than for Allāh's sake, but knowledge insisted on being for Allāh's sake alone." He said in reply:

This saying is erroneous as far as the saints *[awliyāʾ]* of Allāh are concerned, because the acquisition of knowledge other than for Allāh's sake is a form of idolatry *[shirk]*. Let us interpret it in a different sense, assuming that he meant: "[We tried to acquire knowledge for the sake of] the hereafter..." This was also inadequate, so they had to keep working at it, until it brought them to Allāh (Almighty and Glorious is He) and His nearness. They mistook an outer manifestation *[ẓāhir]* for an inner source *[bāṭin]*, a branch for a root. They were seated at the table of the common folk *['awāmm]*, then they were served with the special food of grace. They ate two meals at one sitting. They shared what they received with the common people.

If He wants you to carry out some task, He will equip you for it. If someone really knows how I came to be in this business, yet he stays aloof from me, that person is an offender against the truth *[ḥaqīqa]*.

To anyone who happened to catch sight of him during some kind of supernatural experience *[kharq al-'āda]*, a manifestation of charismatic gifts *[karāmāt]*, one of the saints would say: "You saw that! Come, give me your hand!" Then he would make him promise, with Allāh as his witness, that he would not tell about it until death.

What a miserable wretch is a man who works for a few days for the sake of Allāh, until a secret comes to him from Allāh one night and he tells about it the next day! He must be out of his mind! By Allāh, the man is one thing, and the knowledge *['ilm]* and the charismatic gift *[karāma]* are something else again. One who has such a gift is commanded to keep it a secret, until the judgment *[qaḍā']* and decree of destiny *[qadar]* bring it into the open, while his heart is in safekeeping and his innermost being *[sirr]* is with the Lord of Truth (Almighty and Glorious is He).

If it should ever happen that your heart is tempted by the beauty and charm of this world, you must get away from it in a hurry, for it will no doubt chase after you.

A question was raised. Someone said to the Shaikh: "Weaning is difficult." He said:

For you! Because weaning is difficult only for a baby who is aware of his mother but recognizes nothing else at all. As for one who is capable of understanding, and who has learned how to eat and drink, he loses interest in the milk that comes out of a teat, as if through the eye of a needle.

By Allāh, you must hurry and make for the door! Perhaps you will be numbered among His saints *[awliyā']* and His dear friends *[aṣfiyā']*. Maybe He will arrest it [this world], so that it cannot catch up with you until your heart is no longer troubled by it, until the very memory of it has departed from your heart, and it is left in distress at having lost you for ever. Your love for the King will replace your love of this world. Then eventually, when your heart has been filled with the love of your Lord and His intimate friendship, and when the instruments of control can no longer affect you, this world will be brought back as a maidservant, along with a suit of armor for you to wear and an escort of guards and watchmen. With all her venom now taken from her, she will address you with a loving tongue, saying: "Your allotted portion *[qism]* is in this particular place and that particular place. The daughter of so and so is destined to be your bride...." She will flatter you more and more with every moment that passes.

O people of 'Irāq! O people of the kingdom of this world, of its kings, its costumes and its governors! I have clothes hanging in a wardrobe; you are welcome to any of them you would like to wear! You had better seek safety with me; unless I provide you with soldiers, you lack the power to guarantee it. That is all I have to say to you *[wa's-salām]*.

Renunciation is abstinence *[zuhd]*, while receiving is real experience *[ma'rifa]*... (Stop repeating the teachings *[aqāwīl]* of those who belong to the past. Each one is the Shaikh of his own age.) ...and the abstainer *[zāhid]* is the servant of the one with real experience *['ārif]*.

As long as there is still some kind of lingering interest in this world and its contents and also in the hereafter, as long as there is any kind of residue of natural impulse *[ṭabʿ]* and passion *[hawā]*, how can you really claim to have experienced that renunciation? If one's heart receives whatever it must receive until all that stuff has departed from it, until it has all been pulled out by the roots, then abstinence will be over and done with. Real experience *[maʿrifa]* will have arrived. Pure serenity *[ṣafāʾ]* will have arrived. Murky confusion will be no more. Nearness will arrive. The Lord of Truth will arrive. The Originator *[Musabbib]* will arrive. The material means *[sabab]* will cease to operate. At this point, the person will be restored to a normal condition *[thabāt]*. He will sit at the entrance to His palace, telling his fellow creatures what they must do and what they are not allowed to do.

Your sins become attached to you. Your enemies are thirsting for revenge. If you wish to get the better of your enemies, repent at once and attend to your life hereafter. Allāh is a witness over you, for He is with you whichever way you may turn.

Ibn ʿAṭāʾ[23] used to make this supplication: "O Allāh, have mercy on my exile in this worldly life of mine!"

Death is twofold. There is the death of the common folk *[ʿawāmm]*, which is death as we all know it. There is also the death of the special few *[khawāṣṣ]*, which is the death of the passions *[ahwiya]*, the lower selves *[nufūs]*, the natural urges *[ṭibāʿ]* and the ordinary habits of behavior *[ʿādāt]*. Then, [after this special kind of death,] the heart will be revived. When the heart has been revived, nearness [to the Lord] will come. Once nearness has arrived, everlasting life *[al-ḥayāt ad-dāʾima]* will come. When someone has reached this point, a veil is drawn between him and the memory of death. This experience is granted to his inner being *[bāṭin]*, even while his outer being *[ẓāhir]* is reminding people of death and he, for all external purposes, is remembering it along with them.

I see that your outer selves *[ẓawāhir]* bear witness to the [divine]

[23] Abu'l-ʿAbbās Aḥmad ibn Muḥammad ibn Sahl ibn ʿAṭāʾ al-Ādamī was a close companion of al-Junaid. He was put to death in A.H. 309/922 C.E.

Oneness *[waḥdāniyya]*, while your inner beings *[bawāṭin]* are doing the very opposite of this. I see that your faces are turned in the direction of the Ka'ba [as if you were performing your prayers], while your hearts are directed toward the dirham [silver coin] and the dīnār [gold coin].

If someone feels afraid [of the dangers he must face], he will get on the road before nightfall. Where is your sense of danger? O Allāh, grant salvation *[khalāṣ]*! The devil of the heart that is isolated among the creatures on Allāh's earth (Exalted is He) will come along meekly, with his hands tied.

When you remember Him, you are a lover *[muḥibb]*. When you hear Him remembering you, you are a loved one *[maḥbūb]*. When you remember Him with your tongue, you are a penitent *[tā'ib]*. When you remember Him with your heart, you are a spiritual traveler *[sālik]*. When you remember him with your innermost being *[sirr]*, you are one who really knows *['ārif]*.

It is incumbent upon you to correct the bad aspects of your character before you keep company with the righteous *[ṣāliḥūn]*. Otherwise, as long as you can be influenced by any morsel or scrap, you are not fit to join them, since it would do more harm than good for you to be in their company. You must give up these frivolous habits. Make no one but Him the object of your affection. Make friends with no one but Him. Open your feelings to no one but Him.

You are so perverse, O most wicked of the wicked! O stupid fool! Any Jew *[Yahūdī]* or Christian *[Naṣrānī]* is dearer to you than I am! An impostor *[dajjāl]* comes from Khurāsān; he looks nice and clean on the outside and presents himself to you as an expert in Islamic jurisprudence *[yatafaqqahu]*, and he is dearer to you than I am!

O servants of Allāh, will you not come to everlasting life, to a spring that will never run dry, to a door that will never be locked? Come to a protecting shade that will never pass away, to fruit that will never be in short supply!

> None knows its explanation except Allāh. (3:7)

Oh, what it takes to correct the tendency to satisfy the appetites and desires of the flesh! Oh, what it takes to correct the tendency to indulge in crazy fantasies!

The really good things *[al-khair]* lie beyond your present reach. You must be consumed by the fire of the sincerity *[ṣidq]* of our purpose *[irāda]*, then you will penetrate through all the obstacles and doors. No veil will then be left between us and you. You will see Him as clearly as you can see us. That is when the portions allotted by destiny *[aqsām]* will be made available.

O you who lay claim to saintship *[wilāya]*, do not make such a pretentious claim, because it is a flag hoisted over your head, a herald announcing your arrival. Saintship is a matter of deeds, not words. It is an inner building and its structure is the connectedness *[ittiṣāl]* of the heart. Its keys are faith *[īmān]*, and the reality *[ḥaqīqa]* of it is something about which you do not have a clue.

You must cling to the coattails of one of a special few, that handful of His servants whose lower selves *[nufūs]* have been tamed, and you must not seek anything trivial from them, so that they can make it possible for you to wear their clothes and stand in their presence. Provided you keep this up, he may eventually draw you close, let you try on a few fragments of his sayings, and give you an insight into some of his spiritual states *[aḥwāl]*. Your inner feeling *[ja'sh]* will become steady and your situation will improve. Then, when you come to experience the visitations *[mawārid]* of the Lord of Truth to your heart, you must shut your eyes and be humble. You must not divulge the guide's secret to anyone else.

The visitation *[wārid]* of the Lord of Truth comes to their hearts in various ways, according to their spiritual states *[aḥwāl]* and stations *[maqāmāt]*. They go through outer changes because of the transformations they experience inwardly. The disciple who gets to know their secrets needs to be blind, deaf and intoxicated. Then eventually, when his noble character has become obvious to his guide, when his good behavior has been confirmed by his ability to keep a secret, perhaps the guide will clothe his heart with some of his own garments. While he is praying *[yad'ū]* to Allāh with his outer being *[ẓāhir]*, his heart will be like Joshua *[Yūsha']* the son of Nūn in the company of Moses (may Allāh's blessings be upon them both).[24]

O young man! What is not in your possession *[mulk]* is outside of your domain *[mamlaka]*. The only possibilities are that it belongs to you or that it belongs to someone other than you. In other words, it is either your allotted share *[qism]* or it is the share allotted to someone other than you. If it belongs to you, it will surely come to you, even while you are asleep. So why should you go to all this trouble, to the detriment of your religion *[dīn]*? If only you would make a regular practice of listening in order to acquire knowledge *['ilm]*, and of spending your time in the company of people devoted to religion *[dīn]*, real experience *[ma'rifa]* and the contemplation *[tafakkur]* of that which is to come, it would soon be a simple matter for you to detach yourself from material means and the people who control them *[al-asbāb wa'l-arbāb]*.

To give up working for the sake of creatures, after [one has become capable of] sincerity *[ikhlāṣ]*, is a form of hypocrisy *[riyā']*. As for the case where someone gives up paying attention to creatures in order to gain sincerity, this is expected of him.

As long as you are still a disciple *[murīd]*, you must constantly practice this law *[ḥukm]*. It may be that your practice *['amal]* will lead you to knowledge *['ilm]*. This will employ your heart, the limbs and organs of your physical body, and also your innermost being *[sirr]*. Knowledge will tell you what you must do and what you are not allowed to do.

O Allāh, there is not one amongst us who does not wish for You, but evil influences keep us away from You.

The commandments of Allāh (Almighty and Glorious is He) are a debt *[dain]* you must settle. If you put off paying when you have the ability to do so, you are guilty of injustice *[ẓalamta]*, and if you forswear the obligation, you are guilty of unbelief *[kafarta]*.

[24] Although not mentioned by name in the Qur'ān, Yūsha' ibn Nūn is identified by some Islāmic authorities as the servant referred to in Sūra 18:60: "And when Moses said to his servant: 'I will not give up until I reach the point where the two oceans meet, though I march on for ages.'"

Take from this world in proportion to your need, not for idle sport and to accumulate great wealth. When your Islām becomes real through submission *[taslīm]*, you will surrender *[sallamta]* your own self *[nafs]* to the hand of His destiny *[qadar]*. He will clothe your heart, then He will clothe your outer *[ẓāhir]* and your inner *[bāṭin]*. You will die on such and such a day, then He will bring you back to life. Then He will rid you of bad qualities and impurities.

Whenever he [the believer] looks to creatures, he dies, and whenever he looks to the Lord of Truth, he thrives. When he looks to creatures, he is impoverished, humiliated and despised; he is swallowed by the everyday world. But when he looks to the Lord of Truth, he thrives, recovers his vitality and grows in stature. He is absent from creatures, from his own self *[nafs]* and from his worldly existence *[wujūd]*. He lives with the Truth *[Ḥaqq]* and dies to the creation *[khalq]*.

The record *[kitāb]* of genuine disciples [is kept by the angels]. Whenever a disciple *[murīd]* comes to them, they order him to eliminate something: to eliminate creatures and the self *[nafs]*, then to eliminate this world and the hereafter. Then, when this has been accomplished and he been turned inside out, the Lord of Truth will mold him as He wishes. If you would dearly love to progress to this station *[maqām]*, you must give up things that are unlawful *[ḥarām]* or dubious *[shubha]*. Then, once you have done this completely, you must give up that which is commonly considered lawful *[ḥalāl mushtarak]*. Then you must give up that which is plainly permissible *[mubāḥ]*. Then you must confine yourself to that which is absolutely lawful *[ḥalāl muṭlaq]*, namely that on which there is a consensus *[ijmā']* of both law *[ḥukm]* and knowledge *['ilm]*, a consensus of the outer *[ẓāhir]* and the inner *[bāṭin]*. This applies to that which is not subject to ownership *[malaka]*, like what is to be found in the wastelands and deserts and on the beaches. It will come to you when you are far from having any expectation or concern about it. It will come to you bit by bit while you are asleep. You will open the eyes of your heart to see that you are surrounded by the angels *[malā'ika]* and the spirits *[arwāḥ]* of the Prophets *[nabiyyūn]*, and intuition *[ʿilm]* will advise you to accept it, vouching for the fact that you enjoy the security of nearness [to the Lord].

Have nothing more to do with creatures. Be indifferent to their hopes, to their praise and their blame, to their outer forms *[ṣuwar]* and their inner contents *[maʿnā]*. The grace of Allāh will bring you renewed vitality *[intiʿāsh]*. Then you will be granted nearness and sufficiency, constant companionship, remoteness from the realm of creation and transcendence beyond worldly existence *[fanāʾ ʿani'l-wujūd]*. You must seek annihilation *[maḥw]* after substantiation *[ithbāt]*, nonexistence *[ʿadam]* after existence *[wujūd]*, nearness *[qurb]* after remoteness *[buʿd]*, purity *[ṣafāʾ]* after impurity *[kadar]*, contact *[waṣl]* after separation *[qaṭ]*, rediscovery *[liqāʾ]* after loss *[faqd]*, wholeness of the heart without a tongue, wholeness of the innermost being *[sirr]* without a heart, wholeness of the innermost being without existence.

> There, protection belongs only to Allāh, the True. (18:44)
>
> Then, when He wills, He resurrects him. (80:22)

[He restores him to life] among fellow creatures, and through him He improves the welfare of His servants, and through him He brings them near [to Himself].

O vanity, O crazy foolishness! You must cut off the material means *[asbāb]* and cast off those who control them *[arbāb]*, then you will reach your destination. All that you have left behind will be waiting to greet you. There you will find every kind of food on a platter. You will find the physician in the abode of the Beloved, in the abode of nearness.

A man got up to ask the Shaikh (may Allāh be well pleased with him) a question, but he told him:

Hold your tongue! I see that your question arises from your natural impulse *[ṭabʿ]* and your lower self *[nafs]*. Do not gamble with me. I am an executioner. I am deadly.

And Allāh warns you to beware of Himself. (3:28)

As for you, O common man *['āmmī]*, Allāh is warning you to beware of His chastisement. In your case, O member of the élite *[khāṣṣ]*, Allāh is warning you to beware of Himself. And you, O élite of the élite *[khāṣṣ al-khāṣṣ]*, Allāh is warning you to beware of the transformations He can bring about. He is warning you, O common man, that He is going to take away your hearing, your sight, your energies, your property and your family, then He will transport you to the hereafter, where you will receive your punishment. O élite of the élite, He is warning you to beware of Him, so you must be on the alert to avoid being caught off guard, then the Lord of Truth will whisper to your innermost being *[sirr]*: "I am indeed Allāh. Do not feel afraid or wary."

Once you have experienced the full reality of this, if you ever approach the brink of fear He will pull you back from it, and if your sense of security is ever disturbed by fear, He will make it calm and clear again. Once the heart is completely whole and sound, it can no longer be harmed by anything in the entire realm between heaven and earth. But this is not the kind of thing that can come about through cultivating a nice appearance, daydreaming and affectation *[takalluf]*. This calls for an aptitude that comes from heaven. Active work *[fi'l]*, combined with maintaining abstinence in your heart, will cause you to make progress. Mercy *[raḥma]* will descend upon you, and on your fellow students *[ahl majlisika]*. Positive results and increasing benefits will follow in rapid succession.

A disciple came to a wise man *[ḥakīm]*, sat down in front of him and said: "I would love to own a plot of land in the Garden [of Paradise]. That is all I am seeking." The wise man said to him: "If only it took as little to keep you satisfied in this world, as it will take to ensure your satisfaction in the hereafter!"

Since death is a matter of fact, there can be no way of avoiding it, so you may as well die right away! A corpse has no social relations, nothing to give or withhold, nothing to look forward to, no hostility or friendship to deal with; only stillness and silence. You must be like a corpse in relation to the procurement of benefit and the prevention of harm. The corpse is incapable of speech, but then, if He so wills, He will cause you to speak, even though you are dead. Once you have died to your fellow creatures and to you, the statements you utter will be entirely veracious and true, because the dead can only communicate truth *[ḥaqq]* and veracity *[ṣidq]*.

In response to a written note from a man, a Ṣūfī who wanted something, the Shaikh said:

This is absurd! The Ṣūfī is free from attachment *[yaṣfū]* to creatures; he pays no attention to them. The Ṣūfī is sought, but he does not seek.

A man said to him: "When 'the hole is too wide for the patcher' [as the popular saying goes], what should he do?" He replied:

He should sit in a quiet and receptive state, until destiny *[qadar]* hands him a patch to fit the hole, or mends it in some other way. If you have lost the key, you must sleep by the door, on the threshold.

You are the slave of creatures. You grow fat when they take notice of you, and get thin when they ignore you. You are doomed. You are guilty of associating partners with Allāh *[mushrik]*. Your heart is devoid of the affirmation of His Oneness *[tawḥīd]*. You are the slave of creatures. You are devoid of anything good. You are off the list altogether; you are not listed with the scholars *['ulamā']*, not with those who seek *[murīdūn]*, not with those who are sought *[murādūn]*, and not with the righteous *[ṣāliḥūn]*. If it were not for my sense of shame, I would come to the door of each and every one of you and impose on his hospitality. I would twist his ear, correct his behavior and give him an education.

Oh, the love of this little coin *[dānaq*; one sixth of a *dirham]*! Where does it lead someone who gives it all his attention, who gets involved with it?

Woe unto you! You want me to offer you this world, although it is in the East while I am in the West! I simply accept my own allotted shares *[aqsām]* in it with the affirmation of Divine Unity *[tawḥīd]*. From me you should seek the hereafter and the nearness of the Lord of Truth (Almighty and Glorious is He).

The walls of the religion *[dīn]* of Muḥammad (Allāh bless him and give him peace) are caving in, and its foundations are being scattered about. Come, O people of the earth, let us reconstruct what has been ruined, let us build up that which has collapsed. This is something that will never be completely finished. O sun! O moon! O day! Come hither!

The best part of a spiritual state *[ḥāl]* is that which is kept secret. Let us pretend to be asleep, as we await the arrival of the divine decree *[qadar]*. In the Name of Allāh *[bismi'llāh]*...

Then the Shaikh leaned against the lectern, resting his head on his hand and closing his eyes. He stayed there for a little while, then sat down and said:

You are idiots and lunatics! Your avoidance of me is a capital loss, for which there is no excuse. Do not indulge in fantasy. Do not let your mischief and insolence and impudence get the upper hand over you. You will very soon be dead.

Present at the Shaikh's meeting *[majlis]* on this occasion was the superintendent *[ustādh]* of the household of Imām 'Izzu'd-dīn, the son of the Commander-in-Chief *[ra'īs ar-ru'asā']*, accompanied by numerous servants and attendants. He had never been present at any of his meetings before this one; in fact he had never met him before. When he made his entrance, the Shaikh (may Allāh be well pleased with him) said:

You are all serving one another. Allāh—who will serve Him? You are all mere creatures. Such is the nature of existence *[wujūd]*. O corpse! O dust! You will turn to dust. Your grave will be trampled underfoot. Dust to dust! From the cradle *[mahd]* to the grave *[laḥd]*, you never have a clue; the material means *[sabab]* is always in the way. You are deaf. You suffer from a mental disorder *[khabal]*. You are afflicted with insanity *[junūn]*. Wake up now, before death brings you to your senses! Be your own preacher and subdue your lower self *[nafs]*! Spread your wealth around! You are merely a traveler passing through.

> When their time comes, they can neither put it back an hour, nor bring it forward. (10:49)

All that you possess will turn against you. All those who honor you will turn against you. All those who treat you with respect will turn against you. Your true friend is he who warns you to take care, while your enemy is he who eggs you on.

O Allāh, awaken us from the slumber of the negligent! Make us helpful to one another! Keep our attention on us and on You, so that we may correct our lower selves *[nufūs]* and guide them to you, and so that we may have work to do for the rest of our lives!

Before you can preach to others, there is a necessary precondition to be met: you must be a believer *[mu'min]*. It is not proper for the servant to summon his fellow creatures to the Lord of Truth before having personally attained to Him. You must not ask others to follow you in blind imitation. Woe to the traitor who betrays himself, his Lord and his Prophet; who issues commandments but does not carry them out; who issues prohibitions but does not observe them; who speaks but does not put his own words into practice. You may adopt a humble posture, trim your mustaches and make your face look pale, but none of this is really important. Faith *[īmān]* is here. (He was addressing these remarks to a group of people who were attending to the superintendent of the palace.) This is how they are. Every single one of the people of Allāh has a police force *[shiḥna]* to protect his heart; they combat the lower self *[nafs]*, the natural urges *[ṭab']*, the passions *[hawā]* and highway robbers *[quṭṭā' aṭ-ṭarīq]* on the road to Allāh.

Our Prophet Muḥammad (Allāh bless him and give him peace) has said:

> I saw groups of people whose lips were being clipped off with scissors, so I said: "Who are these?" He said: "The learned scholars *['ulamā']* of your community *[umma]*."

O Allāh, improve us all *[aṣliḥi'l-kull]*! O Allāh, make us righteous *[ij'alnā ṣāliḥīn]* and make us instruments of righteousness *[aṣliḥ binā]*! Let all our needs be left to You, and let our devotion be to You alone!

Come here and lay your hand on my hand—(He is addressing these words to the superintendent of the household of Imām 'Izzu'd-dīn)— so that we may hurry off to our Lord, away from this ruined house, from your property and your children, and escape to Allāh, to the real work!

You must soon return to the Lord of Truth, who will ask you about your deeds. He created you for the purpose of affirming His Oneness *[tawḥīd]*; He did not create you for the sake of this world, nor for the sake of the hereafter. This world can neither satisfy your hunger nor quench your thirst. It is deceitful and cunning. Your tragedy is due to the attention you pay to your lower self *[nafs]*. Your fascination with the superficial aspect of this world is due to the controlling influence of your lower self and the fact that you treat it as a minister *[wazīr]* in charge of your affairs. The believer *[mu'min]* is a manager *[mudabbir]*, not a dodger *[mudbir]*. If you become detached from your lower self, your heart will speak to you. Then the innermost being *[sirr]* will relate to you both. Then the Lord of Truth (Almighty and Glorious is He) will befriend you both. Thus you will come to be the commandant of people and places *[shiḥnatu'l-'ibādi wa'l-bilād]*.

[You may well ask:] How can I depose this lower self *[nafs]*? When you see an Elder *[shaikh]*, you must say: "Here is someone who worshipped Allāh before I existed, and He is worshipped by the righteous *[ṣāliḥ]* and the sinful *[fāsiq]*, by the juvenile and the minor." This is how the lower self will get to be deposed, and this world will be squeezed out of your heart.

The eye of your heart will catch sight of the hereafter, then it will make you notice the door of His nearness, the door of His power *[sulṭān]*, the door of His glory *[kibriyā']* and His majesty *[jalāl]*. The hereafter will seem insignificant to the eyes of your heart. You will yearn for Him and long to meet Him. You will look at this world and regard it as the strangest of all the creatures of Allāh, so it will leave your heart and you will be like a woman who is granted a divorce *[muṭallaqa]* after the discovery of defects [in her marriage partner]. The lower self *[nafs]* will turn away from this world, then the hereafter will present itself in its finest attire, so destiny *[sābiqa]* will show up its faults and point to the fact that it is only an invention *[muḥdatha]*, a created entity *[makhlūqa]*, which the Jews *[Yahūd]* and the Christians *[Naṣārā]* share with you. If they submit *[aslamū]* [to the will of God], there, in the Garden [of Paradise] that is unalloyed and pure, is the nearness of the Lord of Truth (Almighty and Glorious is He), intimate friendship and contact with Him.

Pay no attention to these crazy fools. They were ignorant about this world, so they went off in search of it. They were ignorant about the hereafter, so they went off in search of it. They were ignorant about creatures, so they placed their confidence in them.

O people of ours, be on your guard! Allāh (Exalted is He) told one of His Prophets *[anbiyā']* by means of inspiration *[awḥā]*:

> Be on your guard! Let Me not catch you unawares!

Jacob (peace be upon him) would first weep over Joseph, then he would weep again over himself. He could see in him the signs of his being a Prophet *[nabī]*, and he feared for his chastity *['iṣma]* because he was so handsome and good-looking.

> Deaf, dumb, blind, so they do not understand. (2:171)

You have ears in your heads, but your hearts have no ears. O logs for the Fire [of Hell], O common herd, O rabble! You are in a state of delusion.

> Do not all things come home to Allāh? (42:53)

Am I not a shepherd for you, a cupbearer for you, a watchman for you? I would not have advanced to this point, had I seen you as having any capacity for causing harm and benefit. It was only after I had cut off all attachments with the sword of the affirmation of Divine Unity *[tawḥīd]* that I secured this spiritual station *[maqām]*. Your praise and your blame, your acceptance and your rejection are equally unimportant as far as I am concerned. It so often happens that a person is very critical of me, but then his criticism turns into praise. Both the blame and the praise come from Allāh, not from him. The attention I pay to you is for the sake of Allāh, and anything I receive from you is also for the sake of Allāh. If He empowered me to do so, I would enter the grave with each and every one of you, and I would respond on your behalf to the questions put by [the interrogating angels] Munkar and Nakīr, out of compassion and sympathy for you.

When Allāh loves one of His servants, He fills his heart with ecstasy *[wajd]* and an ardent longing *[shawq]* for Him. Abū Yazīd al-Bisṭāmī was driven into exile seven times, on account of the strange utterances he was heard to make. The doors of nearness are opened to the hearts of servants like these. There is nothing to connect them with ordinary creatures, except their [observance of] the five prayers *[aṣ-ṣalawāt al khams]* and the surname linking them to the family of Adam *[al-ādamiyya]*, to the human race *[al-bashariyya]*. Their bodily forms are the bodily forms *[ṣuwar]* of ordinary human beings, but their hearts are with the decree of destiny *[qadar]* and their innermost beings *[asrār]* are in the company of the King.

As for you, your worshipful obedience is all over your face, your clothes and your outer self *[ẓāhir]*, while your heresy *[zandaqa]* is practiced in your private space, and your unbelief *[kufr]* is all over your inner being *[bāṭin]*. Your heart is laden with hypocrisy *[nifāq]*, arrogant pride *[ʿujb]* and ill-will *[sūʾ aẓ-ẓann]* toward your fellow creatures. Nothing can purify you but the sword, unless you repent. The sacred law *[sharʿ]* commands us to hold our tongues, to be discreet and keep secrets to ourselves, otherwise I would denounce you and have you taken away. I would grab you by the sleeve and drag you outside.

Our words affect your outer *[ẓāhir]*, while our hearts affect your inner beings *[bawāṭin]*. If anyone accuses me of falsehood and calls me a liar, Allāh will show him to be the liar. Allāh will separate him from his dependants, his property and his country, unless he repents.

It never comes around to the time for prayer *[ṣalāt]* without my resolving to go off and leave those who pray in public, but when the moment actually arrives, I am always brought back to join the prayer. It is just the same whenever it is time for a session *[majlis]*.

> Our Lord, do not lay upon us more than we have the strength to bear. (2:286)

Rather than rejoicing with those who are happy, you should be grieving with those who are sad. Rather than laughing with those who are laughing, you should be weeping with those who are shedding tears.

Travel with high aspirations *[himam]*. Consume your allotted portions *[aqsām]* at His door, on the threshold of His nearness.

Have you no common sense? To put it simply, you must turn your back on this world. If you have dependants to provide for, take from it for their sake, not for your own. The Messenger (Allāh bless him and give him peace) used to collect the alms *[ṣadaqāt]* in order to distribute them to the poor, the needy and those engaged in combat *[mujāhidūn]*. Then he would visit his wives' apartments, saying: "Has any divine gift been granted *[futiḥa]*? Has anything come for us?" If the answer was no, he would then say: "In that case, I am fasting *[ṣā'im]*." From the fact that He was withholding His bounty, he understood that Allāh wanted him to fast.

It is like this also with the saints *[awliyā']* of Allāh. One of them may be intending to go up onto the roof of his house, in order to sleep where the heat is less suffocating, but if he sees a door on the stairs, he will understand that he is required to sleep inside his house. If he sees the door of his house standing open, he will understand that he is required to go out into the deserts and the wilderness, so out he will go.

Prophethood *[nubuwwa]* is still here among His creatures. Its traces, its beneficial influence and its inner content *[ma'nā]*, are distributed among the hearts of the saints *[awliyā']*. Prophethood was a kind of food and drink, the leftovers of which remain for the people [of the Lord].

Begone from my presence, O consumers of forbidden food *[ḥarām]* and usurious profit *[ribā]*! I am not a judge *[qāḍī]*. I am one who gives training in the realization of Divine Unity *[tawḥīd]* and sincere devotion *[ikhlāṣ]*. What am I to do with the majority of you? You are a useless lot. Your deeds are proclaimed in your faces, be they good or bad. It is better to hold your tongue and wait, then perhaps your face will be wiped clean; maybe your private life will be transformed and the dirt will be wiped from your face.

A man, one of the people of this city, had just come back from the Pilgrimage *[ḥajj]*. When he came to see me, I said to him: "Turn in repentance to Allāh (Almighty and Glorious is He)." "I have just been on the Pilgrimage," said he, so I told him: "I am aware of that, but then there was sexual misconduct *[zinā]*, sinful and immoral behavior!" He did not repent, however, and when he died I saw him in a vision. While I was performing the funeral prayer over him, he appeared to leave the coffin *[tābūt]* and cling to the hem of my garment, so I said to him: "This is what I tried to warn you about!"

You tell so many lies and make so many false claims. You have a Shaikh and he is there for your benefit, so let it be up to him to give you a record that carries some weight, in case you are deficient in piety and goodness, for this will be read at the time of death, at the moment of separation.

I must hope for your intercession *[shafā'a]* on that day, for this is attributing partners to Allāh *[shirk]*. An affirmation of Divine Unity *[tawḥīd]* that I have practiced since childhood, I am losing today. A door that was open to me, I am slamming shut against me. I have forsaken you all. I deserve neither love nor respect.

A man screamed during his meeting *[majlis]*, and cried: "Allāh!" The Shaikh (may Allāh be well pleased with him) then said: "You will be questioned about this. You will be called to account for it. Why did you speak? Was it ostentation *[riyā']* or hypocrisy *[nifāq]*, sincerity *[ikhlāṣ]* or blasphemy *[shirk]*? This day is a sledge-hammer *[fiṭṭīs]*! If anyone wishes to leave, he may do so, and if anyone wishes to stay, let him stay." Then he uttered a cry and many people got up and approached him, crying and weeping in repentance.

Just then, a sparrow came and settled on his head; so he bowed his head for it. He stayed in that position, with the bird on his head and the people on the stairs of the lectern. He did not stir until one of his companions held out his hand toward it and it flew away. Then he offered a prayer of supplication. The people were making a great commotion with their weeping, supplications and professions of repentance. He stepped down and went out immediately to the congregational mosque *[jāmi']* of ar-Ruṣāfa, followed by a great throng of people, amid a scene of weeping, screaming, ecstasy *[wajd]* and the shedding of clothes. Then he said (may Allāh be well pleased with him): "This is the end of the age. O Allāh, we take refuge with You from the evil thereof!"

Something beckons to me and I would prefer to run away from it, but it is in keeping with the divine judgment *[qaḍā']* and the decree of destiny *[qadar]*.

Do not let this world make off with your religion *[dīn]*. You must preserve your integrity. Earn enough to deal with your pressing concerns. This is the doorway to receiving from Allāh. You must be satisfied with Him and independent of His creatures. The material means *[sabab]* must appeal to the Originator *[Musabbib]*, the outer *[ẓāhir]* to the inner *[bāṭin]*. The weary toil is over and done with, or, in the case of something about to be started and embarked upon, one will be told: "Come, let us go the Originator. Let us go to the source. Let us go to the root. Let us knock at the doors of the divine judgment and the decree of destiny. Let us stop at the door of knowledge *[ʿilm]*, at the head of the valley of gracious favor *[wādi'l-faḍl]*, there to settle down and make ourselves at home. Sufficiency *[kifāya]* and providence *[ʿināya]* have now arrived. Right guidance *[hidāya]* has arrived. Direct experience *[maʿrifa]* has arrived. All forms of knowledge *[ʿulūm]* have arrived. We have many different doors through which to enter His presence. You must conduct yourself properly."

Ibrāhīm al-Khawwāṣ (may Allāh bestow His mercy upon him) once said: "I spent several days in a desert, where I did not see a soul, then my journey led me to a place that gave me a very weird feeling. Suddenly, I came upon a young man standing there. I wondered what to make of him, so I asked him: "Where do you come from?" He said: "[From] Him." Then I asked him: "Where are you going?" and he said: "[To] Him." "If you are telling the truth," I said to him, "let yourself be a sacrifice *[fidā']* for Him." At this he uttered a cry and fell down, so I went up close to him—and saw that he was dead. I then left him out of range of my sight, as I went off to gather pebbles to make him a burial mound, but when I came back to the spot, I did not find him there. Then I heard a mysterious voice *[hātif]* calling: "O Ibrāhīm, the angel of death *[malak al-mawt]* came looking for this same person, but he could not find him. The Fire [of Hell] came looking for him, but it could not find him." So I asked: "Where is he now?" and the mysterious voice replied:

> Amid gardens and rivers, in a sure abode, in the presence of a Mighty King. (54:54,55)

O crazy fools, you must not be so careless!

> Enter houses by the proper doors. (2:189)

[Enter] by the doors of the Shaikhs, by the doors of those whose whole existence has become absorbed in obedient service to Allāh

(Almighty and Glorious is He). They have become formless contents *[ma'ānī]*. They have come to be the boon companions *[jalīsūn]* of the house of nearness [to the Lord]. They have come to be the guests of the King. On one story [of His palace] they are offered food, and on another they are offered rest and relaxation. Robes of honor of many kinds are provided for them to change into. He takes them on a tour of His kingdom, His earths and His heavens, His mysteries and His intimate knowledge *[ma'rifa]*.

You are behind a wall that is over three miles [one *farsakh*] thick, and yet all you have with you is a needle, so how can you possibly make a hole through it? When the people [of the Lord] come to that wall, a thousand doors are opened for them, and each of those doors invites them to enter through it.

Accept the benefit *[ni'ma]* and flee to the Benefactor *[Mun'im]*. It must not put you under an obligation, so leave it with someone to whom you are indebted. Look closely at the 'benefit': Is it a blessing, or is it a curse *[niqma]*, or is it truly a mercy *[raḥma]*? Do not be deceived by its external appearance. Do not forget the Benefactor because of it. Look neither to the right nor to the left. Never let your eyes turn aside from the Benefactor.

Do not accept food from the hand of this world, for it may well be poisoned. If it brings you food, check with your two ministers, the Book and the Sunna. You must accept their mutually agreed recommendation *[mashwara]*, so if they both advise against it, you had better hesitate. Do not act in haste. Do not be greedily impatient.

Ask your own self *[nafs]* for its opinion, even if the legal experts *[muftūn]* have offered you theirs. If you struggle against the lower self and refuse to comply with its demands, it will eventually be fused together with the heart. The two will become one single entity. It will be addressed and summoned:

> O self now at peace *[yā ayyatuha'n-nafsu'l-muṭma'inna]*! (89:27)

It will come to receive information from the heart, while the heart receives information from the innermost being *[sirr]*, and the innermost being receives information from the Lord of Truth (Almighty and Glorious is He).

Give pious caution *[waraʿ]* its due, then eat and do not worry about it. Give dutiful devotion *[taqwā]* its due, then eat and do not worry about it.

The Shaikh (may Allāh the Exalted be well pleased with him) also said:

We are Your pilgrims *[ḥujjāj]*, Your seekers *[quṣṣād]*, Your aspirants *[murīdūn]*, Your applicants *[ṭullāb]*, Your lovers *[muḥibbūn]* and Your petitioners *[ṭālibūn]*. Our children, our families and our homes have been left behind, so do not disappoint us! To be preoccupied with anything other than Allāh (Almighty and Glorious is He) is weary toil; with the lower self *[nafs]* it is sinful disobedience, and with creatures it is deviation from His door.

There are some among the saints *[awliyāʾ]* before whom the angels *[malāʾika]* bow down in prostration, with their hands tied behind their backs. A few individuals among the saints can see the angels. One of these was that righteous man *[ṣāliḥ]* who was sitting hungry in a mosque *[masjid]* in Damascus, when he said to himself: "If only I knew the Supreme Name *[al-ism al-aʿẓam]* of Allāh!" Two figures immediately came down from above and sat by his side. One of them said to the other: "Do you wish to know the Supreme Name of Allāh?" "Yes," he replied, so the first speaker said to him: "Say 'Allāh!' " [The man said:] "I said to myself: 'I say that.' " Then [the angel] said: "That is not the way to say it. We want you to say 'Allāh' while there is nothing other than Him in your heart." Then, [said the man:] "The pair of them rose up into the sky before my very eyes."

Assign your outer being *[ẓāhir]* to the creation and your heart to the hereafter. As for your innermost being *[sirr]*, you must lodge it with the Lord of Truth, beyond both this world and the hereafter. If you are capable of this, [well and good,] but if not, you are not ready to enjoy security. You must flee to the wastelands and the wilderness. You must acquire faith *[īmān]* in isolated places, in the deserts and the wilderness, then you may come back among your fellow creatures. You must look for a companion *[rafīq]* in your isolation, before taking the road back to creatures.

After some discussion, the Shaikh (may Allāh be well pleased with him) went on to say:

They collect. They distribute to others, they share. They operate in accordance with the inner purpose *[ma'nā]*. They are making you a charitable gift by collecting from you. The aspirant *[murīd]* collects from Allāh (Almighty and Glorious is He), while he who has real experience *['ārif]* collects from creatures. The one with real experience collects from them because he is the agent *['āmil]*, the expert *[jahbadh]*, the deputy *[nā'ib]* of the King. He collects from creatures for the sake of others, not for himself, and his office is with the King, in His presence and behind doors and screens. His personal desires *[shahawāt]* are beneath his feet, and he also keeps creatures underfoot.

The staff of Moses (peace be upon him) swallowed everything up, yet it did not alter or change. If you cannot succeed at my hand, you will never achieve success *[falāḥ]*. I do not teach you for the sake of your rank, and I shall not hesitate to use the stick on you through being afraid of your worldly power *[sulṭān]* and influence *[saṭwa]*. Any business that distracts your attention from me is inauspicious for you. Your bad luck will soon affect your dependants, and they will have to go begging. The righteous man *[ṣāliḥ]* entrusts his dependants to Allāh and commits them to His safekeeping. As for the immoral hypocrite *[munāfiq]*, his dependants must rely on his dirham and his dīnār [his money] and whatever legacy he leaves them from his real estate and his business. Their ultimate fate will undoubtedly be a state of poverty. You are ignorant, despicable, an accursed outcast, for you have sown in your heart the love of the [golden] calf of this world.

O Allāh, support him who seeks this world in order to sustain himself in the practice of religion *[dīn]*, as well as him who seeks the hereafter for the sake of Your countenance. But do not support him who seeks the hereafter for the sake of appearances only, and do not support him who seeks this world for this world's sake, because both of these represent separation from You.

If only one of you can achieve salvation, we shall be clinging to his coat tails tomorrow [at the Resurrection]! When a righteous man *[ṣāliḥ]* comes to me, I say to him: "If you have anything for tomorrow, take us with you as your companions, and mention us in your prayer of supplication *[daʿwa]*. And if we have anything, we shall let you have a share in it."

Accept my words as candid, without ulterior motive, then you will prosper. If this is indeed correct, both you and I stand to gain. If the opposite is true, then you will be the winner and I shall be the loser.

Creatures are of three kinds: Angel *[malak]*, devil *[shaiṭan]* and human *[ins]*. The angel is wholly good. The devil is wholly evil. The human is mixed, a blend of good and evil, so if the good predominates he is connected to the angel, and if the evil predominates he is linked to the devils *[shayāṭīn]*.

O my people! Islām is weeping and crying out for help. It is holding its head in its hands because of all these dissolute types *[fujjār]*, these immoral sinners *[fussāq]*, these promoters of heretical innovation and error *[ahl al-bidaʿ wa'ḍ-ḍalāl]*; because of the tyrants *[ẓalama]*; because of those who dress up in the clothes of falsehood; because of those who lay claim to qualities they do not possess. Consider your predecessors and those you once had with you, commanding and forbidding, eating and drinking—it seems as though they never were!

How hard is your heart *[qalb]*! A dog *[kalb]* will serve its master faithfully in the hunt, in his fields, with his livestock and when required to keep watch, and at the sight of him it will happily wag its tail. Yet he only gives it a morsel or a few morsels to eat for supper, or feeds it something quite insubstantial, whereas you consume the blessings of Allāh and eat your fill of them, without giving Him the results He has a right to expect, without fulfilling His due. You refuse to obey His commandments. You do not observe His guidelines *[ḥudūd]*.

O young man! You must not value anything as highly as poverty *[faqr]*, patience *[ṣabr]* and salvation *[salāma]*. Be completely satisfied with Allāh in your poverty, for the rich man tends to exceed the proper limits and forget his Lord. He prefers the life of this world. He gives his own whims and passions *[hawā]* priority over the commandment of Allāh. He puts the lower self *[nafs]* and natural impulse *[ṭab']* before the commandment of Allāh. He prefers breaking fast *[fiṭr]* to fasting *[ṣawm]*. He prefers the unlawful *[ḥarām]* to that which is lawful *[ḥalāl]*. He prefers absent-mindedness to vigilant wakefulness. He prefers sinful disobedience to repentance.

Woe unto you! Your private parts *[saw'a]* are uncovered. Shame on you!

The Prophet (Allāh bless him and give him peace) is reported as having said:

> That you should learn about a man by hearsay is better than that you should approach him, and that you should approach him is better than that you should get to know him well, for once you get to know him well you are likely to despise him and despise his work.

This age is pathetic. Most people present you with a baffling conundrum *[ulqiyya]*: A hole on the outside revealing one on the inside; a padlock on a building in ruins; rotting floorboards that are useless for anything but firewood.

In this world the believer *[mu'min]* is a king, and in the hereafter he is also a king. He practices obedience to Him, and he gives up disobeying Him. He affirms His Oneness *[waḥḥadahu]* in private and in public. He despises this world and leaves it like a repudiated woman, who implores him from behind his back: "O my dear son, take your food and drink!" To this he responds by saying: "I shall not eat until I reach the door of the hereafter. Maybe it is poisoned, mother dear! Set aside what you have there with you, until the lady superintendent *[qahramāna]* of the hereafter comes along. When she has come and inspected your food, when she has tasted it and sniffed it, then and only then will I eat from her hand."

[Like a great lady,[25]] the hereafter will take you to her [the *qahramāna* in charge of her household], and she will give you her own food to eat and her own drink to quench your thirst. A door will be shut to keep this world out.

While you are in this situation, the hand of [divine] jealousy will make you bow down in glorification *[subḥa]* of your Lord. The hand of His Majesty will be upon you, [and He will ask:] "What is this reliance on something other than Me? Is it not a creature? Is it not a product of creation? Why did you not come to Me, rather than to the palace?" After he has taught you, clothed you, entertained you, administered the antidote *[tiryāq]* to you and equipped you with the armor of helpful guidance *[tawfīq]*, pious caution *[wara']* and protection *[ḥifẓ]*, you will eventually go forth into this world in His company. He will build you a platform *[dikka]* so that you can address the people of both this world and the hereafter.

What is the matter with you? What do you make of Him? He will not let you catch even a slight fever. Death will approach you and He will drive it away, so it may be postponed for a while.

Stick close to the men of Truth *[rijāl al-Ḥaqq]*. They have some crazy people *[majānīn]* to attend to, people immersed in the ocean of this world. They treat the sick, rescue the drowning and have compassion for those in torment.

[25] In Arabic, the words *ad-dunya* [this world] and *al-ākhira* [the hereafter] are grammatically feminine. This makes it easy for an Arabic speaker or writer to personify them as female beings — a 'woman' and a 'lady' in these passages — if he wishes to represent them as characters in a parable, rather than as abstract entities.

Be near to such a person, if you can recognize him. If you cannot recognize him, then you are by yourself.

Destiny *[qadar]* smiles on those who are content with the [divine] judgment *[qaḍā']*. It takes them by the hand and leads them to the King. It asks for the door to be opened unto them and brings them near to the King. At this point they become members of the party *[ḥizb]* of Allāh. This is no mere fantasy. The basis for this is perfectly sound. They comply with the decree of destiny. They do not quarrel with it and they do not contest it. Harmony, harmony *[muwāfaqa muwāfaqa]*!

Yaḥyā ibn Mu'ādh once said: "The words of the champions of truth, the representatives of the Messengers *[kalām aṣ-ṣiddīqīna 'l-qā'imīna maqāma 'r-rusul]* and their deputies *[abdāl]* entrusted with their secrets, are inspiration *[waḥy]* from Allāh. What they have to say is authorized by Allāh *['ani'llāh]*, comes through Allāh *[bi'llāh]* and is about Allāh *[fi'llāh]*."

Sit in a graveyard. Speak to the dead and ask them: "What have you experienced? What has become of you? Where is the family? Where are the children? Where are the houses? Where are the possessions? Where is the youth? Where is the strength? Where are the commandments? Where are the prohibitions? Where is the taking? Where is the giving? Where are the friends? Where are the desires of the flesh?" They will seem to be telling you: "We feel regret for what we have left behind, but we are also happy with what we sent on ahead."

If you wish to visit the places of burial, you must be quite alone and unaccompanied, and make sure that no other visitors, women or men, are present there.

Be sensible! All of you will soon be dead.

One day a funeral procession *[janāza]* came in during his meeting *[majlis]*, so the Shaikh said:

Can you not see this dead man at the moment death came for him, when it startled him and made him lose his senses, so that he was aware of nothing apart from his Lord (Almighty and Glorious is He)?

Obituary of the Shaikh

(may Allāh be well pleased with him!)

ʿAbd al-Wahhāb spoke with his father the Shaikh (may Allāh be well pleased with him) during his death sickness, asking him for some good advice. He responded (may Allāh be well pleased with him) by saying:

"You must observe your duty *[taqwā]* to Allāh and practice obedience to Him. Fear no one and pin your hopes on no one [but Him]. Entrust all your needs to Allāh (Almighty and Glorious is He), and look to Him to supply them. Do not put your trust in anyone apart from Allāh (Almighty and Glorious is He). Do not rely on anyone but Him (Glory be to Him). The affirmation of His Oneness; the affirmation of His Oneness; the affirmation of His Oneness *[at-tawḥīd at-tawḥīd at-tawḥīd]*. All is contained within the affirmation of His Oneness."

He also said during his death sickness:

"When the heart is whole and sound in relation to Allāh (Almighty and Glorious is He), it wants for nothing and loses nothing. I am a kernel *[lubb]* with no shell."

He also said to his sons:

"Keep your distance from me, for I may be with you outwardly *[bi'ẓ-ẓāhir]*, but inwardly *[bi'l-bāṭin]* I am in the company of others. Between me on the one side, and you and all creatures together on the other, there is a distance equal to the distance between heaven and earth, so do not compare me with anyone and do not compare anyone with me."

He also said (may Allāh be well pleased with him):

"Others besides you have come into my presence, so make room for them and treat them courteously. A very great kindness here. You must not crowd their space."

One of his sons also told me that he kept saying:

"And on you be peace, and Allāh's mercy and His blessings *[wa-'alaikumu's-salām wa-raḥmatu'llāhi wa-barakātuhu]*! May Allāh forgive me and you, and may Allāh relent toward me and toward you. In the Name of Allāh, farewell!"

He said this for a day and a night. He also said:

"Woe unto you! Nothing worries me, no angel, not even the angel of death *[malak al-mawt]*. O angel of death! He who cares for us has blessed us with something beyond you." Then he uttered a loud cry. This was what happened during the day in the late evening of which he died.

One of his sons asked him how he was feeling, but he said:

"Let no one ask me about anything. I am basking in the knowledge *['ilm]* of Allāh (Almighty and Glorious is He)."

He also said to his son 'Abd al-Jabbār:

"Are you asleep or awake? Die in relation to me, then you may come to your senses."

I entered his presence when a group of his offspring were with him, and his son 'Abd al-'Azīz was writing from his dictation. He said: "Get a disinterested person *['afīf]* to write for him," so I took [a pen] and I wrote:

"After hardship, Allāh will surely grant ease. (65:7)

"Give instructions for details to be reported as they happened. The law *[ḥukm]* may be subject to change, but knowledge *['ilm]* is unchanging. The law may be abrogated, but knowledge is never abrogated. Allāh's knowledge is not altered by His law."

His sons 'Abd ar-Razzāq and Mūsā told me that he would often raise his hand and stretch it out, while saying:

"And on you be peace, and Allāh's mercy and His blessings! Repent and join the ranks. That is when I shall come to you."

He would also say: "Be gentle, be gentle *[irfaqū irfaqū]*!"

Then he experienced the moment of Truth *[al-Ḥaqq]* and the agony of death *[sakrat al-mawt],* as he was saying:

"I seek help in [the words]: 'There is none worthy of worship but Allāh, the Ever-Living *[al-Ḥayy],* the Self-Sustaining *[al-Qayyūm],* the One who never dies and has no fear of passing away. Glory be to Him who exults in His omnipotence, and subdues His servants with death. There is none worthy of worship but Allāh *[lā ilāha illa'llāh].* Muḥammad is Allāh's Messenger *[Muḥammadur-rasūlu'llāh].*"

His son Mūsa told me that when he was trying to say the word *ta'azzaza* ["exults"], he could not get his tongue around the correct pronunciation, so he kept on repeating *"ta-'az-za-za"* over and over again, slowly and emphatically, until his tongue got it right. Then he said: "Allāh, Allāh, Allāh..," until his voice grew faint and his tongue was cleaving to the roof of his mouth. Then he died. May Allāh be well pleased with him and grant him contentment! May He reunite us with him "in a sure abode, in the presence of a Mighty King" (54:54,55).

Praise be to Allāh, Lord of All the Worlds *[wa'l-ḥamdu lillāhi Rabbi'l-'ālamīn]*, and Allāh's blessings *[ṣalawāt]* be upon the Chief of the Prophets *[sayyid al-anbiyā']* and the Captain of the Intercessors *[muqaddam ash-shufa'ā']*, Muḥammad, the Best of Mankind *[khair al-barriyya]*—may Allāh bless him and his family and all his companions!

Concerning the Author, Shaikh ʿAbd al-Qādir al-Jīlānī

A Brief Introduction by the Translator[1]

The Author's Names and Titles

A rich store of information about the author of these *Utterances* is conveniently available, to those familiar with the religious and spiritual tradition of Islām, in his names, his surnames, and the many titles conferred upon him by his devoted followers. It is not unusual for these to take up several lines in an Arabic manuscript, but let us start with the short form of the author's name as it appears on the cover and title page of this book: *Shaikh ʿAbd al-Qādir al-Jīlānī.*

Shaikh: A term applied throughout the Islamic world to respected persons of recognized seniority in learning, experience and wisdom. Its basic meaning in Arabic is "an elder; a man over fifty years of age." (The spellings *Sheikh* and *Shaykh* may also be encountered in English-language publications.)

ʿAbd al-Qādir: This is the author's personal name, meaning "Servant [or Slave] of the All-Powerful." (The form *ʿAbdul Qādir,* which the reader may come across elsewhere, is simply an alternative transliteration of the Arabic spelling.) It has always been a common practice, in the Muslim community, to give a male child a name in which *ʿAbd* is prefixed to one of the Names of Allāh.

[1] Reproduced for the convenience of the reader, with slight modifications from the version printed on pp. xiii–xix of: Shaikh ʿAbd al-Qādir. *Revelations of the Unseen (Futūḥ al-Ghaib).* Translated from the Arabic by Muhtar Holland. Houston, Texas: Al-Baz Publishing, Inc., 1992.

al-Jīlānī: A surname ending in *-ī* will often indicate the bearer's place of birth. Shaikh 'Abd al-Qādir was born in the Iranian district of Gīlān, south of the Caspian Sea, in A.H. 470/1077-8 C.E. (In some texts, the Persian spelling *Gīlānī* is used instead of the arabicized form *al-Jīlānī*. The abbreviated form *al-Jīlī,* which may also be encountered, should not be confused with the surname of the venerable 'Abd al-Karīm al-Jīlī, author of the celebrated work *al-Insān al-Kāmil,* who came from Jīl in the district of Baghdād.)

Let us now consider a slightly longer version of the Shaikh's name, as it occurs near the beginning of *Al-Fatḥ ar-Rabbānī* [The Sublime Revelation]: *Sayyidunā 'sh-Shaikh Muḥyi'd-Dīn Abū Muḥammad 'Abd al-Qādir (Raḍiya'llāhu 'anh).*

Sayyidunā 'sh-Shaikh: "Our Master, the Shaikh." A writer who regards himself as a Qādirī, a devoted follower of Shaikh 'Abd al-Qādir, will generally refer to the latter as *Sayyidunā* [our Master], or *Sayyidī* [my Master].

Muḥyi'd-Dīn: "Reviver of the Religion." It is widely acknowledged by historians, non-Muslim as well as Muslim, that Shaikh 'Abd al-Qādir displayed great courage in reaffirming the traditional teachings of Islām, in an era when sectarianism was rife, and when materialistic and rationalistic tendencies were predominant in all sections of society. In matters of Islamic jurisprudence *[fiqh]* and theology *[kalām],* he adhered quite strictly to the highly "orthodox" school of Imām Aḥmad ibn Ḥanbal.

Abū Muḥammad: "Father of Muḥammad." In the Arabic system of nomenclature, a man's surnames usually include the name of his first-born son, with the prefix *Abū* [Father of—].

Raḍiya'llāhu 'anh: "May Allāh be well pleased with him!" This benediction is the one customarily pronounced—and spelled out in writing—after mentioning the name of a Companion of the Prophet (Allāh bless him and give him peace). The preference for this particular invocation is yet another mark of the extraordinary status held by Shaikh 'Abd al-Qādir in the eyes of his devoted followers.

Finally, we must note some important elements contained within this even longer version: *al-Ghawth al-A'ẓam Sulṭān al-Awliyā' Sayyidunā 'sh-Shaikh Muḥyi'd-Dīn 'Abd al-Qādir al-Jīlānī al-Ḥasanī al-Ḥusainī (Raḍiya'llāhu 'anh).*

al-Ghawth al-A'ẓam: "The Supreme Helper" (or, "The Mightiest Succor"). *Ghawth* is an Arabic word meaning: 1. A cry for aid or succor. 2. Aid, help, succor; deliverance from adversity. 3. The chief of the Saints, who is empowered by Allāh to bring succor to suffering humanity, in response to His creatures' cry for help in times of extreme adversity.

Sulṭān al-Awliyā': "The Sultan of the Saints." This reinforces the preceding title, emphasizing the supremacy of the *Ghawth* above all other orders of sanctity.

al-Ḥasanī al-Ḥusainī: "The descendant of both al-Ḥasan and al-Ḥusain, the grandsons of the Prophet (Allāh bless him and give him peace)." To quote the Turkish author, Shaikh Muzaffer Ozak Efendi (may Allāh bestow His mercy upon him): "The lineage of Shaikh 'Abd al-Qādir is known as the Chain of Gold, since both his parents were descendants of the Messenger (Allāh bless him and give him peace). His noble father, 'Abdullāh, traced his descent by way of Imām Ḥasan, while his revered mother, Umm al-Khair, traced hers through Imām Ḥusain."

As for the many other surnames, titles and honorific appellations that have been conferred upon Shaikh 'Abd al-Qādir al-Jīlānī, it may suffice at this point to mention *al-Bāz al-Ashhab* [The Gray Falcon].

The Author's Life in Baghdād

Through the mists of legend surrounding the life of Shaikh 'Abd al-Qādir al-Jīlānī, it is possible to discern the outlines of the following biographical sketch:

In A.H. 488, at the age of eighteen, he left his native province to become a student in the great capital city of Baghdād, the hub of political, commercial and cultural activity, and the center of religious learning in the world of Islām. After studying traditional sciences under such teachers as the prominent Ḥanbalī jurist *[faqīh]*, Abū Sa'd 'Alī al-Mukharrimī, he encountered a more spiritually oriented instructor in the saintly person of Abu'l-Khair Ḥammād ad-Dabbās. Then, instead of embarking on his own professorial career, he abandoned the city and spent twenty-five years as a wanderer in the desert regions of 'Irāq.

He was over fifty years old by the time he returned to Baghdād, in A.H. 521/1127 C.E., and began to preach in public. His hearers were profoundly affected by the style and content of his lectures, and his reputation grew and spread through all sections of society. He moved into the school *[madrasa]* belonging his old teacher al-Mukharrimī, but the premises eventually proved inadequate. In A.H. 528, pious donations were applied to the construction of a residence and guesthouse *[ribāṭ]*, capable of housing the Shaikh and his large family, as well as providing accommodation for his pupils and space for those who came from far and wide to attend his regular sessions *[majālis]*.

He lived to a ripe old age, and continued his work until his very last breath, as we know from the accounts of his final moments recorded in the Addendum to *Revelations of the Unseen*.

In the words of Shaikh Muzaffer Ozak Efendi: "The venerable 'Abd al-Qādir al-Jīlānī passed on to the Realm of Divine Beauty in A.H. 561/1166 C.E., and his blessed mausoleum in Baghdād is still a place of pious visitation. He is noted for his extraordinary spiritual experiences and exploits, as well as his memorable sayings and wise teachings. It is rightly said of him that 'he was born in love, grew in perfection, and met his Lord in the perfection of love.' May the All-Glorious Lord bring us in contact with his lofty spiritual influence!"

The Author's Literary Works

Al-Ghunya li-ṭālibī ṭarīq al-ḥaqq **[Sufficient Provision for Seekers of the Path of Truth].** Arabic text published in two parts by Dār al-Albāb, Damascus, n.d., 192 pp. + 200 pp. English translation commissioned for eventual publication by Al-Bāz Publishing, Inc.

In his own introductory remarks, Shaikh 'Abd al-Qādir explains how he came to compose this monumental work: "One of my friends had been pressing me, urging me in very emphatic terms to compose this book, because of his excellent appreciation of what is right and proper... I came to recognize the sincerity of his wish to acquire real knowledge of modes of behavior consistent with the sacred law..., real knowledge of the Maker (Almighty and Glorious is He)..., instruction in the Qur'ān and Prophetic utterances, and real knowledge of the morals and ethics of the righteous. All of these subjects we shall review in the course of the book, so that it may serve as a helper to him in following the path of Allāh (Almighty and Glorious is He), in carrying out His commandments and observing His prohibitions."

Al-Fatḥ ar-Rabbānī **[The Sublime Revelation].** A collection of sixty-two discourses delivered by Shaikh 'Abd al-Qādir in the years A.H. 545-546/1150-1152 C.E. Arabic text published by Dār al-Albāb, Damascus, n.d. Arabic text with Urdu translation: Madīna Publishing Co., Karachi, 1989. English translation: Shaikh 'Abd al-Qādir al-Jīlānī. *The Sublime Revelation (Al-Fatḥ ar-Rabbānī).* Translated from the Arabic by Muhtar Holland. Houston, Texas: Al-Baz Publishing, Inc., 1993.

Even a non-Muslim scholar like D.S. Margoliouth was so favorably impressed by the content and style of *Al-Fatḥ ar-Rabbānī* that he wrote:[2] "The sermons included in [this work] are some of the very best in Muslim literature: the spirit which they breathe is one of

[2] In his article "'Abd al-Ḳādir" in *Encyclopaedia of Islam* (also printed in *Shorter Encyclopaedia of Islam.* Leiden, Netherlands: E.J. Brill, 1961).

charity and philanthropy: the preacher would like to 'close the gates of Hell and open those of Paradise to all mankind.' He employs Ṣūfī technicalities very rarely, and none that would occasion the ordinary reader much difficulty..."

Malfūẓāt **[Utterances of Shaikh 'Abd al-Qādir].** Frequently treated as a kind of appendix or supplement to manuscript and printed versions of *Al-Fatḥ ar-Rabbānī.*

Futūḥ al-Ghaib **[Revelations of the Unseen].** A collection of seventy-eight discourses. The Arabic text, edited by Muḥammad Sālim al-Bawwāb, has been published by Dār al-Albāb, Damascus, 1986. German translation: W. Braune. *Die Futūḥ al-Ġaib des 'Abd al-Qādir.* Berlin and Leipzig: Walter de Gruyter & Co., 1933. English translations: 1. M. Aftab-ud-Din Ahmad. *Futuh Al-Ghaib [The Revelations of the Unseen].* Lahore, Pakistan: Sh. Muhammad Ashraf. Repr. 1986. 2. Shaikh 'Abd al-Qādir al-Jīlānī. *Revelations of the Unseen (Futūḥ al-Ghaib).* Translated from the Arabic by Muhtar Holland. Houston, Texas: Al-Baz Publishing, Inc., 1992.

Jalā' al-Khāṭir **[The Removal of Care]** or ***Jalā' al-Khawāṭir*** **[The Removal of Cares].** A collection of forty-five discourses by Shaikh 'Abd al-Qādir. Arabic text with Urdu translation, under title *Jalā' al-Khawāṭir,* published by Maktaba Nabawiyya, Lahore, n.d.

Other works attributed to Shaikh 'Abd al-Qādir include short treatises on some of the Divine Names; litanies *[awrād/aḥzāb];* prayers and supplications *[da'awāt/munājāt];* mystical poems *[qaṣā'id].*

May Allāh forgive our mistakes and failings, and may He bestow His blessings upon all connected with our project—especially our gracious readers! Āmīn.

Muhtar Holland

About the Translator

Muhtar Holland was born in 1935, in the ancient city of Durham in the North East of England. This statement may be considered anachronistic, however, since he did not bear the name Muhtar until 1969, when he was moved—by powerful experiences in the *latihan kejiwaan* of Subud—to embrace the religion of Islām.*

At the age of four, according to an entry in his father's diary, he said to a man who asked his name: "I'm a stranger to myself." During his years at school, he was drawn most strongly to the study of languages, which seemed to offer signposts to guide the stranger on his "Journey Home," apart from their practical usefulness to one who loved to spend his vacations traveling—at first on a bicycle—through foreign lands. Serious courses in Latin, Greek, French, Spanish and Danish, with additional smatterings of Anglo-Saxon, Italian, German and Dutch. Travels in France, Germany, Belgium, Holland and Denmark. Then a State Scholarship and up to Balliol College, Oxford, for a degree course centered on the study of Arabic and Turkish. Travels in Turkey and Syria. Then National Service in the Royal Navy, with most of the two years spent on an intensive course in the Russian language.

In the years since graduation from Oxford and Her Majesty's Senior Service, Mr. Holland has held academic posts at the University of Toronto, Canada; at the School of Oriental and African Studies in the University of London, England (with a five-month leave to study Islamic Law in Cairo, Egypt); and at the Universiti Kebangsaan in

* The name Muhtar was received at that time from Bapak Muhammad Subuh Sumohadiwidjojo, of Wisma Subud, Jakarta, in response to a request for a suitable Muslim name. In strict academic transliteration from the Arabic, the spelling would be *Mukhtār*. The form *Muchtar* is probably more common in Indonesia than *Muhtar*, which happens to coincide with the modern Turkish spelling of the name.

Kuala Lumpur, Malaysia (followed by a six-month sojourn in Indonesia). He also worked as Senior Research Fellow at the Islamic Foundation in Leicester, England, and as Director of the Nūr al-Islām Translation Center in Valley Cottage, New York. His freelance activities have mostly been devoted to writing and translating in various parts of the world, including Scotland and California. He made his Pilgrimage *[Ḥajj]* to Mecca in 1980.

Published works include the following:

al-Ghazālī. *On the Duties of Brotherhood.* Translated from the Classical Arabic by Muhtar Holland. London: Latimer New Dimensions, 1975. New York: Overlook Press, 1977. Repr. 1980.

Sheikh Muzaffer Ozak al-Jerrahi. *The Unveiling of Love.* Translated from the Turkish by Muhtar Holland. New York: Inner Traditions, 1981. Westport, Ct.: Pir Publications, 1990.

Ibn Taymīya. *Public Duties in Islām.* Translated from the Arabic by Muhtar Holland. Leicester, England: Islamic Foundation, 1982.

Hasan Shushud. *Masters of Wisdom of Central Asia.* Translated from the Turkish by Muhtar Holland. Ellingstring, England: Coombe Springs Press, 1983.

al-Ghazālī. *Inner Dimensions of Islamic Worship.* Translated from the Arabic by Muhtar Holland. Leicester, England: Islamic Foundation, 1983.

Sheikh Muzaffer Ozak al-Jerrahi. *Irshād.* Translated [from the Turkish] with an Introduction by Muhtar Holland. Warwick, New York: Amity House, 1988. Westport, Ct.: Pir Publications, 1990.

Sheikh Muzaffer Ozak al-Jerrahi. *Blessed Virgin Mary.* Translation from the Original Turkish by Muhtar Holland. Westport, Ct.: Pir Publications, 1991.

Sheikh Muzaffer Ozak al-Jerrahi. *The Garden of Dervishes.* Translation from the Original Turkish by Muhtar Holland. Westport, Ct.: Pir Publications, 1991.

Sheikh Muzaffer Ozak al-Jerrahi. *Adornment of Hearts.* Translation from the Original Turkish by Muhtar Holland and Sixtina Friedrich. Westport, Ct.: Pir Publications, 1991.

Sheikh Muzaffer Ozak al-Jerrahi. *Ashki's Divan.* Translation from the Original Turkish by Muhtar Holland and Sixtina Friedrich. Westport, Ct.: Pir Publications, 1991.